MW00835563

A Practical Guide to Cybersecurity in SAP®

Julie Hallett

Thank you for purchasing this book from Espresso Tutorials!

Like a cup of espresso coffee, Espresso Tutorials SAP books are concise and effective. We know that your time is valuable and we deliver information in a succinct and straightforward manner. It only takes our readers a short amount of time to consume SAP concepts. Our books are well recognized in the industry for leveraging tutorial-style instruction and videos to show you step by step how to successfully work with SAP.

Check out our YouTube channel to watch our videos at *https://www.youtube.com/user/EspressoTutorials*.

If you are interested in SAP Finance and Controlling, join us at *http://www.fico-forum.com/forum2/* to get your SAP questions answered and contribute to discussions.

Related titles from Espresso Tutorials:

► Maxim Chuprunov: **Leveraging SAP® GRC in the Fight Against Corruption and Fraud**
http://5216.espresso-tutorials.com/

► Martin Metz, Sebastian Mayer: **Practical Guide to Auditing SAP Systems**
http://5248.espresso-tutorials.com

► Bert Vanstechelman, Chris Walravens, Christophe Decamps: **Securing SAP® S/4HANA**
http://5258.espresso-tutorials.com

► Bert Vanstechelman:**The SAP® HANA Implementation Guide**
http://5289.espresso-tutorials.com

► Tracy Juran: **Beginner's Guide to SAP® Security and Authorizations**
http://5013.espresso-tutorials.com

► Anurag Barua: **Decision-Maker's Guide to SAP S/4HANA Cloud, essentials edition**
http://5424.espresso-tutorials.com

The SAP eBook Library:
Team and Company Access

Did you know that you can provide your team with effective SAP training with access to the SAP eBook Library and reduce travel and training costs? You can!

Curious about how we stack up against the competition?

	Espresso Tutorials	Other Offerings
Price per Year	**$159 annually**	**$699 annually**
SAP eBooks	✓	✓
SAP video tutorials	✓	✗
Mobile app	✓	✓
Immediate access to new titles	✓	✓
Self service to maintain users (for companies)	✓	✗

Pricing available for teams of 5+. A team of 10 can access the library for one year for $850 (pre-tax). That's a 42% discount. The larger your team, the more you save.

Try a free 7-day, no obligation trial:
http://free.espresso-tutorials.com

Get a quote for your team today:
http://company.espresso-tutorials.com

Julie Hallett
A Practical Guide to Cybersecurity in SAP®

ISBN:	978-3-960-12957-8
Editor:	Karen Schoch
Cover Design:	Philip Esch
Cover Photo:	istockphoto.com | ipopba 1165058709
Interior Book Design:	Tanja Jahns

All rights reserved.

1st Edition 2021, Gleichen

© 2021 by Espresso Tutorials GmbH

URL: *www.espresso-tutorials.com*

All rights reserved. Neither this publication nor any part of it may be copied or re-produced in any form or by any means or translated into another language without the prior consent of Espresso Tutorials GmbH, Bahnhofstr. 2, 37130 Gleichen, Germany.

Espresso Tutorials makes no warranties or representations with respect to the content hereof and expressly disclaims any implied warranties of merchantability or fitness for any particular purpose. Espresso Tutorials assumes no responsibility for any errors that may appear in this publication.

Feedback
We greatly appreciate any feedback you may have concerning this book. Please send your feedback via email to: *info@espresso-tutorials.com*.

Table of Contents

Preface

SAP Security is a unique and complex application security environment. As the complexity of the integrated nature of applications, networks, internet and devices continues to accelerate, so have the requirements for securing and protecting SAP.

I began working with SAP after many years as an application programmer, network and systems administrator. This background gave me a deep understanding of how SAP worked from the operating system through to the user experience. As I completed my education in cybersecurity I was able to see the connections between cybersecurity and SAP Security; between cyber risk management and SAP governance and risk management.

The depth and detail required to secure SAP was really uncovered during the initial Sarbanes Oxley remediation requirements for segregation of duties. That 'kicked the rock over', so to speak, and exposed not only the risks involved with SAP access management, but what the risks were for external access or breach. I personally began researching the integration of SAP into a security program in the early 2000's and began speaking on the subject at SAP conferences in the United States. During the evolution of the idea of "cyber"security, I began detailing how SAP fit into a cyber framework and started working with SAP as a partner contributor to their Enterprise Threat Detection software package during its initial research and development processes.

My intention in writing this book is to share that knowledge in language that everyone from the CISO (Chief Information Security Officer) to the analyst can understand and apply to their own environments. This will help in understanding risk when budgeting, purchasing, implementing, hiring, and cloud sourcing, and when outsourcing for SAP, SAP bolt-on applications, and integrated services.

For people who are relatively new to SAP Security, I recommend reading through this entire book to deepen your understanding of the critical components that need to be secured in SAP. For the grizzled SAP Security veteran, the intention of this book is to give you ideas and process improvements, and to improve communication and understanding between the SAP Security and Cyber/Network teams.

Acknowledgements

I'd like to take a moment to thank my family for all their support. I thank my husband for listening to me babble and rant in the cybersecurity language that was often completely foreign to him. A special thanks to my daughter, Sarah Hallett-Reeves who acted as my first-pass editor. A cyber professional in her own right, she spotted errors, but more importantly, caught things that I thought I had put into writing but which were still stuck in my head. Thank you to Espresso Tutorials for their commitment to quality SAP instructional materials.

We have added a few icons to highlight important information. These include:

Tips	
	Tips highlight information that provides more details about the subject being described and/or additional background information.

Examples	
	Examples help illustrate a topic better by relating it to real world scenarios.

Attention	
	Attention notices highlight information that you should be aware of when you go through the examples in this book on your own.

Finally, a note concerning the copyright: all screenshots printed in this book are the copyright of SAP SE. All rights are reserved by SAP SE. Copyright pertains to all SAP images in this publication. For the sake of simplicity, we do not mention this specifically underneath every screenshot.

1 Introduction

The threat matrix is constantly changing. Organizations that understand and respond effectively stay a step ahead of the hackers and protect their critical data. There are clear definitions of what this means in respect to network security, but it is not as clear when it comes to data protection. When data protection is merged with application security, things become even more confusing. Application security is not considered as carefully in the process of hardening network and data security. Applications as complex and interconnected as SAP have to be managed differently than local network or PC-based applications.

Connectivity to SAP has increased and the network firewalls and perimeter no longer defend the application. Cloud connectivity and data enrichment through sales, purchasing, human resource management and other applications in the cloud are new avenues for hackers. Customers, vendors, employees and mobile devices accessing core SAP data, and the need for that data to be available to the internet, have opened new vulnerabilities. This increased risk to corporate intellectual property, customer, vendor, and employee critical data needs to be understood and managed.

This book aims to break down the application of cybersecurity as it applies to SAP into actionable items that can be communicated and brought into existing security frameworks. Cybersecurity as a buzzword will be separated from the multi-layered program reality. Security frameworks will be reviewed and the use of a framework applied at the application layer. External risks to SAP will be defined. The internal security risks in SAP will be identified, and governance and remediation processes detailed.

2 Cybersecurity defined

Cybersecurity is not a simple term. It is a concept, program, and process that encompasses data security as a whole. Understanding the holistic nature of cybersecurity will help to develop the process to bring SAP® into a cyber/data security program.

Cybersecurity has been a major buzzword over the last few years, and will continue to be so in the future. It refers to the technologies, processes, and practices designed to protect networks, computers, programs, and data from attack, damage, and unauthorized access, as defined by the U.S. National Institute of Standards and Technology (NIST). It is not simply another name for security, it is the holistic program that wraps around multiple layers of security, compliance, policy and education.

Stop hackers at the network perimeter

Cybersecurity is much more than a way to stop hackers at the network perimeter. It incorporates all aspects of data security, including the largest threat to security—people: employees, contractors, and customers.

A *cybersecurity program* is a holistic processing of requirements and tasks across all layers (see Figure 2.1). It results in a communications chain that manages change across all areas of the IT organization. The goal of the program is to ensure each layer takes into account the other areas impacted by new and emerging threats, and to change implementation.

Creating a holistic data security plan requires a well-thought-out and planned cybersecurity program. In this diagram, the layers of the program are nested and sized according to their importance, level of potential risk, and difficulty to manage. *Network security* receives the most publicity in cybersecurity discussions, but it only plays a small part and depends on the other layers from the perspectives of education, execution, and governance.

13

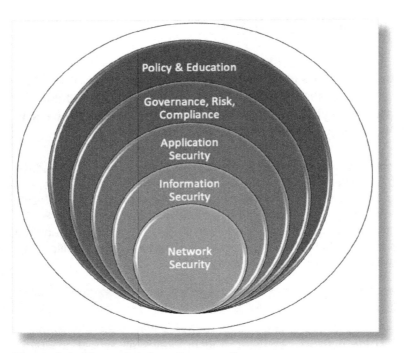

Figure 2.1: Elements of a cybersecurity program

Policy and education is the largest and most complex layer of a cyberse-curity program. Definition, socialization and enforcement of policy has legal implications across the entire organization. Security education often requires customization for company divisions, job levels, departments and risk levels, according to the data being managed. This includes the delivery methods for the curriculum, enforcement of education, and recertification on an annual basis. Once employees are educated, regular updates and education about new threats need to be delivered to each employee. The policy and education layer is the foundation of all governance and com-pliance efforts, applications, information and network security.

Governance, risk and compliance in the cybersecurity program is not a reference to the SAP GRC module (also called Governance, Risk and Compliance). Here, it refers to the processes of managing overall risk to the information, data, intellectual property, and systems that belong to a company. This includes monitoring and enforcing policy, education require-ments, threat identification and response, business continuity planning and disaster recovery.

Managing compliance to regulatory requirements for the corporate location and business space means keeping up with all the latest regulations such as the European Union General Data Protection Regulation (GDPR), the NIST CIS (Center for Internet Security) Controls, and the Cybersecurity Maturity Model Certification (CMMC) that are currently being implemented by the US Government as of 2020, as well as many other regulation and certification requirements. The requirements of these regulations permeate through all layers of a cybersecurity program generating new policy, education, application and information security requirements and classifications as well as network security processes.

Application security includes office automation applications, access to network shared drives and data stores, business automation applications, human resources applications, research and development, and many others. Each application has access to data through specific data-storage locations. Access to display or maintain that data needs to be given, while also being careful to provide only the minimum amount of access needed for task requirements. Many companies default to a model where they give their users access to everything they might need at any point in time in order to reduce future access requests and minimize interruption to task execution. Access models are often copied from one group to the next without carefully considering data confidentiality. Designing and implementing application security is time and resource intensive; however, remediation of security after an incident, or for regulatory requirements is much more difficult and can risk business continuity.

Information security includes classification of data into confidentiality tiers. The review and identification of data that is to be restricted is dictated to some extent by regulatory and legal requirements. This includes human resources (HR) data, personally identifiable information (PII), protected health information (PHI) and some company financials. Using this as the only restrictions on corporate information creates risk to the data, thereby impacting a company's trade secrets such as customer lists, price lists, suppliers and supplies, product bills of materials, drawings and assembly details, and new product development. These could be mismanaged and left available to hackers. It is at this level of detail that the intersection between application and information security becomes critical. Unclassified information that is left available to many applications is classified as potential risk. If that data is saved by an employee on an unsecured internet drive (in order to work on it elsewhere), the situation changes from a potential risk to an actual risk, unknown and unmanaged.

These different layers can either reduce or create risk at the network security layer. A breach of policy due to lack of education can introduce new, emerging, or *zero-day* threats to the network. A zero-day threat is a vulnerability that has not previously been discovered or exploited. Zero-day means it is the very first time the vulnerability has been exploited by a hacker. The more access the users have across applications and information stores, the more areas a *threat actor* has to act upon. A threat actor is any person, entity or code that exploits risks or attacks systems. This could include information theft, the planting of malicious code, or the implementation of a robot/bot network application that can launch attacks against other internal targets, external companies, or entities from within the corporate network perimeter.

The use of Shadow IT

 Another example of how all the different layers of a cybersecurity program work together to secure corporate data and assets would be the use of *Shadow IT*—the implementation of a technology solution outside the control of the IT department. This occurs when an internal business team decides to employ a cloud service provider to do data enrichment or other services.

When groups or departments decide to implement an application and access to it, without the knowledge or participation of the company's IT team, the standard information technology policies and processes are circumvented, which is a breach of protocol that introduces multiple layers of risk. The use of this service now introduces new data, network and access management risks when it is not in a managed or approved process. This includes the risk that a terminated employee is not removed from their company's online access. If the user is not removed, they will still be able to access the data, and the credentials of that user are then compromised (especially if users are using the same password everywhere). This creates a network penetration risk. Additionally, issues encountered by the service provider are now risks to the company as a whole.

The connection and communication of the five layers of a cybersecurity program are critical for creating a secure, informed technology environment and for managing risk.

3 Using a security framework to manage risk

A framework is a tool used to identify the right questions to ask, and to understand how to organize that information into manageable standards.

3.1 What is a framework?

A framework is a set of guidelines laid out to create standardization across processes. Frameworks are the tools used to implement standards. The terms *frameworks* and *standards* are often used interchangeably. For the purposes of this chapter, we will use them separately with their common definitions:

- ▶ *Framework*—a basic structure or system of rules underlying a system; a concept that facilitates decision making

- ▶ *Standards*—a rule, principle, technique, process or template designed to provide consistency to planning, development, operation, implementation and governance

A framework is the foundation of questions that guide the creation, understanding, and education of standards and policies. Standards can be self-governing, but the framework provides high level governance to ensure the standards are being met and monitored. Where things get tricky is when there are different frameworks that govern different types of data.

Frameworks are tools to create structure and stability

Frameworks provide a structured set of topics to use to evaluate a system or software. They can be used for any hardware, software, network or data management process to create stability and security.

3.1.1 Frameworks defined

Frameworks are used to streamline operations, processes and audits. The point of a framework is to ask the right questions of the right areas. These questions are not just for the technology but also for the technology consumers and practitioners. Gaps, overlaps and redundancies in processes are often identified while implementing a framework.

The phases of implementation

An implementation or expansion of a framework to include additional systems or areas is done in phases. Each control within the framework requires a question, an answer, documentation, a plan, education, implementation, and governance/audit steps. As you can see, these steps touch on each layer of the cybersecurity program definition we discussed in the previous chapter.

Data Types and Frameworks

The data diagram shown in Figure 3.1 depicts different types of data stored within a network perimeter. For each data type there are different frameworks, governance rules, and internal and external access requirements, as well as different levels of confidentiality. These are like ripples in a pool and intersect with other data types, frameworks and regulatory requirements. To understand this ripple effect, some examples below demonstrate different frameworks/regulations and take a deeper look at a few of the most popular frameworks.

Data type examples include:

▶ *Personally identifiable information (PII)*—names, addresses, and government identification numbers

▶ *Protected health information (PHI)*—health data, diagnosis, and chronic illness data

▶ *Intellectual property (IP)*—any creations of the mind, such as inventions, documentation, designs, and art used in commercial applications

▶ *Financial Data*—corporate profit and loss, and account information

- ▶ *Master Data*—suppliers, supply types, material types, and amounts

- ▶ *Confidential Data*—contract negotiation data, long term planning, and new product development

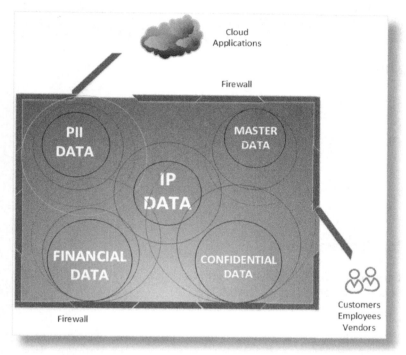

Figure 3.1: Data types and regulations, with overlaps

Examples of regulations are:

- ▶ *HIPAA*—Health Insurance Portability and Accountability Act (USA)

- ▶ *GDPR*—General Data Protection Regulation (EU)

- ▶ *COBIT 2019*—Control Objectives for Information Technologies

- ▶ *NIST CIS Controls*—National Institute of Standards in Technology Center for Internet Security Controls 7.1

- ▶ *CMMC*—Cybersecurity Maturity Model Certification (USA)

- ▶ *SOX*—Sarbanes-Oxley Act (USA), Section 404 (Management Assessment of Internal Controls)

Different data types have different framework and governance requirements. Table 3.1 shows some of the frameworks, with an overlap in the data types.

	PII/PHI data	Financial data	Intellectual property	Master data	Confidential data
CMMC	X	X	X	X	X
COBIT 2019	X	X			X
GDPR	X				X
HIPAA	X				X
NIST CIS CONTROLS	X	X	X	X	X
SOX		X			

Table 3.1: Framework to data type cross reference

3.1.2   Popular frameworks

The most common cybersecurity-focused frameworks in use are the NIST CIS Controls, the GDPR, and the CMMC.

NIST CIS Controls

The National Institute of Standards in Technology Center for Internet Security Controls 7.1 is a prioritized set of recommended practices for securing a wide range of systems and controls. This framework asks questions of all aspects of an organization and is divided into three categories: basic, foundational and organizational.

NIST CIS Controls are evolving

The NIST CIS Controls and cybersecurity frameworkis the most commonly used framework. It is used to institute control, create a plan for improved security and the ability to audit processes. It is constantly evolving so be sure to keep up to date with changes by checking the NIST.gov website for the latest updates.

The *basic* category includes the review of assets, vulnerability management, administrative privileges, secure configurations of hardware, and audit log analysis. These are considered basic and are the highest priority for organizations of any size. An example of a basic category goal is: to maintain an accurate and updated inventory of all technology assets including details of the asset, status of use and connectivity to the network.

The *foundational* category includes email and web browser protection, malware defense, network port and protocol control, data recovery, secure configuration of network hardware, network boundary defenses and data protection. This is the second set of controls implemented due to escalating complexity. An example of a foundational category goal is: to ensure that only fully supported web browsers and email clients are allowed within the organization, with the latest version supplied by the vendor.

The *organizational* category includes security awareness training, application software security, incident management, and penetration tests. This level of control is not needed for smaller companies and requires a more in-depth cybersecurity program. An example of an organizational category goal is: to train workforce members to identify and manage sensitive information.

Key definitions

- ▶ *IGs* (CIS Controls Implementation Groups)—self-assessed categories based on organization size and relevant cybersecurity attributes

- ▶ *Controls*—the first-level category of system or data being managed

- ▶ *Sub-controls*—the second-level detailed goal(s) organized by asset type and security function

Key principles

- ▶ Offense informs defense—the use of information gathered from actual attacks creates the foundation to build an effective defense.

- ▶ Prioritization—implement the controls that bring the greatest risk reduction first.

- ▶ Measurements and metrics—create common metrics in language that is understood by executives, information technology practitioners, auditors and security officials.

▶ Continuous diagnostics and mitigation—continually monitor, measure and validate to ensure quality diagnostic data and mitigating controls.

▶ Automation—automate defense mechanisms to allow the controls to be continuously measured and scaled.

For more information, refer to: *http://cissecurity.org.*

GDPR

The General Data Protection Regulation is a regulatory framework that manages data privacy for the European Union but which has a global impact. Any company collecting personal data for people residing in any European Union country is required to comply with this regulation. At its core definition, GDPR requires data integrity, accuracy, security, and transparency for any personal data gathered, as well as giving the data subject the ability to update their own data or request it be deleted. This means that companies that collect personal data for their use must prove that they keep it safe and must also give data subjects the right to update their data or have it forgotten completely. Historically, once user data was in a list, that data was there forever; it could be bought and sold as a commodity regardless of its accuracy or risk. GDPR addresses those historic principles, placing governance requirements, legal accountability, and fines around data.

GDPR integrates with all other frameworks

 At its core, GDPR does not manage the end-to-end global information technology footprint of a company as other frameworks do, but integrates it into other frameworks. It places privacy requirements at every level of data utilization—gathering the data from the user, coding and processing that data, and storing and managing the data long-term.

Key definitions

▶ *Chapter*—high-level grouping of the different governance classifications

▶ *Articles*—the classification of the provisions include general provisions, principles, rights of the data subjects, etc.

- *Recitals*—the detailed requirements of the article (for example, Article 1—subject-matter and objectives, Recital 1—data protection as a fundamental right)

- *Personal data*—personally identifiable data (name, address, country, etc.)

- *Data processing*—the work being done by the program

- *Data subject*—the data being used by the data processing

- *Data controller*—the person responsible for the personal data use and storage

- *Data processor*—the person that processes personal data at the request of the data controller

Key principles

- Lawfulness, fairness and transparency—the processing and management of personal data must be lawful, fair and transparent

- Purpose limitation—use of the personal data is limited to the reason for which it was collected

- Accuracy—personal data must be kept accurate and up-to-date as much as possible

- Storage limitation—personal data must only be stored for as long as necessary for the purpose it was collected

- Integrity and confidentiality—personal data must be processed and stored in a way that ensures integrity and confidentiality

- Accountability—GDPR compliance must be demonstrable by data processor

Privacy rights

- The right to be informed—the right to know what is being done with data

- The right of access—the ability to know what data is being stored and the ability to change that data

- The right to rectification—the ability to request changes or corrections to stored personal data

- The right to erasure—the right to have your data removed (also known as the right to be forgotten)

► The right to restrict processing—the right to restrict what is being done with personal data

► The right to data portability—the right to move personal data

► The right to object—the right to stop the use of personal data

► Rights in relation to automated decision making and profiling—the right to know what decisions are made through automation without human interaction

For more information, refer to: *https://gdpr.eu/*.

CMMC

The Cybersecurity Maturity Model Certification is a new framework developed by the United States Under Secretary of Defense for Acquisition working with the Department of Defense (DOD), Universities and federally funded research centers. The CMMC framework was developed with the intention of protecting the supply chain for the military and US government, and applies to any company or agency that provides goods or services for the government.

CMMC will create growth in cybersecurity

 The CMMC is a new framework and certification process. There will be tremendous growth in cybersecurity practice implementation in the coming years as it evolves to protect critical infrastructure.

The CMMC was developed in response to cyber threats and breaches within the DOD supply chain that compromised classified and controlled unclassified information. These attacks resulted in the loss of critical intellectual property from suppliers and the use of supplier networks to launch successful and unsuccessful attacks against the defense and supply chain networks.

Key definitions

► *DIB (defense industrial base)*—made up of over 300,000 companies that provide goods and services to the DOD supply chain

► *Cyber hygiene*—practices required to maintain system health and improve security

▶ *Capabilities*—achievements to ensure cybersecurity objectives are met. Each domain is made up of a set of capabilities. There are 43 capabilities.

▶ *Domains*—a set of capabilities that are based on cybersecurity best practices. There are 17 domains within CMMC.

▶ *Processes*—required procedures or activities that are necessary to achieve a capability level. There are five processes across five levels to measure process maturity.

▶ *Practices*—specific technical activities required to achieve a specific level of cybersecurity maturity.

▶ *CMMC level*—there are five levels of cybersecurity maturity measured against specific processes and practices. There are 171 practices across five levels to measure capabilities.

▶ *Maturity model*—a set of indicators that determine progress in a domain and that are auditable against established requirements.

▶ *Certification*—the result of a process audit that validates the execution of practices, resulting in CMMC level validation and certification.

Key principles

▶ Protect federal contract information

▶ Protect controlled unclassified information

▶ Implement standardized and measurable cyber hygiene across the DIB

▶ Implement a certification process and artifact for entities bidding on federal contracts, streamlining the supplier evaluation process. Different levels of maturity are required based on the sensitivity of the information to be protected; the required maturity level escalates for higher levels of data sensitivity.

For more information, refer to: *https://www.acq.osd.mil/cmmc.*

The CMMC provides a framework, or roadmap, for a company to mature its cybersecurity practices through a set of levels (see Figure 3.2). The higher the maturity level, the greater the consideration in the contract bid and retention process. Companies are required to maintain their level certification throughout the entire relationship with the government and submit audit results to prove certification maintenance.

LEVEL 1 PERFORMED	LEVEL 2 DOCUMENTED	LEVEL 3 MANAGED	LEVEL 4 REVIEWED	LEVEL 5 OPTIMIZING
0 PROCESSES	2 PROCESSES	3 PROCESSES	4 PROCESSES	5 PROCESSES
1. Select practices are documented	1. Each practice is documented including lower levels	1. Each practice is documented including lower levels	1. Each practice is documented including lower levels	1. Each practice is documented including lower levels
	2. Policies exist that include all activities	2. Policies exist that include all activities	2. Policies exist that include all activities	2. Policies exist that include all activities
		3. Plans exists for all activities	3. Plans exists for all activities	3. Plans exists for all activities
			4. Activities are reviewed and measured for effectiveness	4. Activities are reviewed and measured for effectiveness
				5. Standardized documented approach across all organizational units

Figure 3.2: CMMC maturity levels

The CMMC provides a cross reference of the most common security frameworks in use for each of its domains in the CMMC Model Appendices. Companies that already use an existing framework can easily see where they need to improve in order to comply with the CMMC.

3.1.3 Which frameworks work best with which SAP modules?

Looking at the six frameworks reviewed in this chapter, the best options are the NIST CIS Controls and the CMMC. These are more comprehensive and better able to address the breadth and depth of data stored and used in SAP. Apart from the SOX regulations, the other frameworks are addressed using either NIST or CMMC. The benefit of the CMMC over NIST is that it comes with a clear plan on what to do to incrementally improve system security. Using NIST CIS Controls or CMMC requires an organized plan, financial investment, and a multi-year implementation to bring SAP into compliance with a framework.

NIST framework widely accepted

 All frameworks can be applied to SAP, but in pracice the NIST model has the maturity and global acceptance by SAP and its integration partners. This acceptance means easier implementation at the customer level.

3.1.4 How does using a framework for security create control?

Using a framework creates control in all the areas in which it is applied. It creates an opportunity and offers the right questions to ask in order to improve the security and processes around SAP. It impacts security, change management, patch application, note application, testing processes, archiving, disaster recovery, user access management, and more. In the next chapter, we will dive into some specifics on how the seemingly vague questions apply to SAP, and how using them improves the risk profile of the landscapes. Once a framework is applied to SAP, it is possible to make measurable assessments of risk and make decisions about the priority of impacts to the SAP landscape.

4 Reconciling SAP cybersecurity to frameworks and regulatory compliance requirements

Reconciling SAP Cybersecurity to frameworks and regulatory requirements involves a cross section of people from SAP Security, SAP Basis server administration, network administration, and business users. Including all these people gives a well-rounded view of the system set-up, and an understanding of how the business uses the different modules. This chapter will walk through the process of evaluating SAP for inclusion in a cybersecurity program.

4.1 Framework and guideline types

In most cases, companies are already using a framework to manage their network risk profiles. When there are multiple options already in place, or if there is no framework in use, deciding on the best framework for SAP starts with a system assessment. Some examples of assessment questions are:

- ► What physical hardware is in use?
- ► What operating system is in use?
- ► What are the server operating system patching policies?
- ► What database is in use?
- ► What are the database patching policies?
- ► Where are the servers located?
- ► What are the internal and external connections and how are they secured?
- ► What version of SAP is in use?
- ► What are the support pack and upgrade policies?
- ► What SAP modules are in use?
- ► What is the criticality of the data stored in SAP?
- ► What is the security role design and change management policy?

▶ Do security roles follow SAP best practices of no manual authorization entries, transactions in a limited number of role suites, roles derived on organizational values?

▶ Are SAP high-risk transactions and authorization objects controlled?

▶ What is the security note application policy?

▶ Are personal devices allowed to connect to SAP and store data?

▶ Where is the user base located?

▶ Are users in countries with high fraud and IP data loss specifically controlled?

▶ What is the user access management policy?

▶ What is the user access review policy?

▶ Is segregation of duties in place and monitored?

▶ Is the SAP HR module in use and is there an HR mini master in place on some servers?

▶ What HR PII/PHI data can be found in SAP?

▶ What bank data for the company, vendors, customers, and employees is stored in SAP?

These questions align with several different frameworks. The key is to look at what frameworks are already in use and line up with the one that covers many of these assessment questions. When these questions start being answered, the data gathered will prompt follow-up questions for additional details and new framework questions.

Auditability moving forward

 Once an assessment is complete, the questions and answers will organically evolve into audit questions that can be asked on an annual basis. It will also be apparent what kinds of document artifacts are needed.

4.2 Steps of a compliance project

Assessment

Using the questions outlined in this chapter, first gather as much information about the systems, network, users, and environment as possible. Ask the follow-up questions and research the current and immerging threats that are applicable to the industry. Compile this information into a few documents and make sure you have current contact information on who to talk to about network, server, policy, business and regulatory requirements.

Evaluation of assessment

Next, categorize the information discovered in the assessment process and begin the evaluation process. To evaluate the assessment information, you need to look for all the issues and information as they line up against the chosen framework or regulation. Use that framework to guide the compilation and categorization of the assessment information.

Using the NIST CIS Controls Version 7.1 as an example, look at the controls and sub-controls to categorize the information gathered in the assessment. Organize the information into the control areas in the framework and begin to review it in that order. If the company is already using this framework, the data from this analysis will eventually be categorized into the risk matrix already in place. For example, here are some assessment questions relating to software patches:

- ▶ What are the server operating system patching policies?
- ▶ What are the database patching policies?
- ▶ What are the support pack and upgrade policies?

Table 4.1 is an example of Continuous Vulnerability Management goals.

Control	Sub-control	Asset type	Security function	Control title	Control description
3	3.4	Applications	Protect	Deploy automated operating system patch management tools	Deploy automated software update tools in order to ensure that the operating systems are running the most recent security updates provided by the software vendor.

Table 4.1: Example of NIST CIS Control

Current state architectural diagram

Once the analysis information is categorized according to the framework being used, a current-state architectural landscape diagram should be created and reviewed. An architectural landscape diagram is a detailed drawing of the network, including all hardware and communications channels. Layered on top of this are any security vulnerabilities uncovered during the assessment. Figure 4.1 shows an example of a high-level architectural diagram created for an assessment.

In this situation, there was no pre-existing architectural landscape diagram. The assessment process gathered enough information to identify internal and external communications, cloud applications and services that housed processes and data, and the types of system users. It also identified elevated levels of risk in communications channels that are overprovisioned, and a lack of security patching being performed.

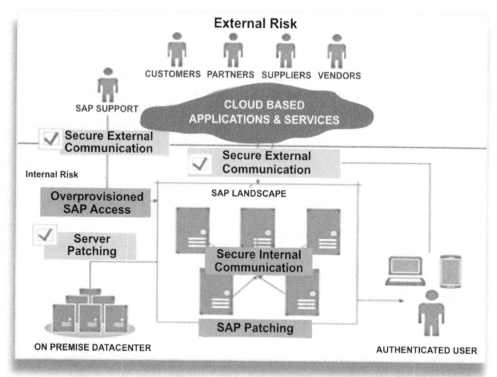

Figure 4.1: Example of a high level architectural diagram

Architectural diagrams and risk

 Many companies do not have an end to end architectural diagram. Each different IT group may have its own. Gathering these and layering them can help identify risk for all of the IT groups. Creating this overarching diagram may require several iterations with input from IT and the business. It will be an invaluable asset in the future for planning, new system implementation and overall risk management.

Gap analysis

The process of categorizing information and diagramming it exposes gaps in the systems and processes. Working through the data generates additional questions to gather information on. This additional evaluation process confirms or clarifies the gaps uncovered. It is important to take these questions back and talk through them with the key stakeholders. This will validate the issue and can be used to pull together information to resolve the gap and further strengthen the documentation.

Policy and procedure evaluation

The next step is to look at the policies and procedures surrounding the different analysis points and gaps. Policies include things such as corporate computer use, mobile device management, and user access review policies. If such policies are not in place, these are now gaps to be added to the evaluation. The IT department needs to review the policies, including assessing what risk categorization process and rating levels are in use, and what the level of risk is.

It is important to ask questions regarding access policies for users in high-risk countries, hiring practices in those countries, and securing network and computer hardware in those countries. The intention is to ensure that there are precautions in place to mitigate higher fraud and risks to intellectual property.

Business requirements review

In performing the data organization and analysis, identifying the business requirements for applications and data clarifies the business necessity for software and user access. For example, does everyone in the procurement department require access to the cloud procurement application, or can this be limited to a few people to reduce the data and access risks? These types of questions clarify how the business uses certain information and how critical it is to the business. If it is regular practice to give a user in the procurement group access to anything and everything that the department has ever utilized, then a gap analysis step needs to be added to review the use of all users on all those systems to determine if it is a critical path. When (or if) a user has ever logged into those systems, how often, and, if possible, what data they use from the systems, need to be reviewed. If only one job title in the department ever logs into that system, then the access for all other users can be terminated until required. This reduces the potential data exposure if a user ID is compromised.

Risk analysis

The categorized and enriched data from the assessment is now ready to have risk analysis performed against it. The risk analysis starts by looking at the gaps and determining how large that gap is, and how many people, systems and amount of data those gaps place at risk. This is a more subjective level of risk analysis that the business and management needs to perform to help further categorize and measure.

Software patching is easier to categorize and prioritize. NIST recommends using the Common Vulnerability Scoring System (CVSS) to evaluate vulnerabilities and risks. Software vendors, including SAP, use this scoring system for identified vulnerabilities and publish them with CVSS scores. This scoring system is outlined in Table 4.2.

Severity	Base Score Range
None	0.0
Low	0.1−3.9
Medium	4.0−6.9
High	7.0−8.9
Critical	9.0−10

Table 4.2: CVSS v3.0 scoring system

More information is available at the National Vulnerability Database (NVD) website: *https://nvd.nist.gov/vuln-metrics/cvss.*

Risk priority assignment for SAP vulnerabilities

SAP Security notes are scored with the above-mentioned ratings system. This rating is important for decision-making regarding note application prioritization. In addition, the note must be reviewed against the business criticality of the systems, processes, and data impacted by the note. The more critical the process and CVSS rating on the note, the higher the risk will be to the business. The note is then weighed against other factors such as:

► Number of systems impacted

► Number of external connections to the system

- ▶ Number of users

- ▶ Internet facing, accepting or sending downloads

- ▶ Risky background users (Remote Function Call (RFC) vulnerabilities)

- ▶ Potential for business interruption or user impact at the transactional level

- ▶ User visibility of the issue

These CVSS ratings and additional risk information are aligned with the company's policies regarding implementing patches based on CVSS rating.

CVSS rating will drive implementation

 Understanding the CVSS rating will drive prioritization of system updates.

Recommendations white paper

The next step is to finalize the assessment information, gap analysis, and risk information, as well as remediation and mitigation recommendations, into a white paper. This paper should be in non-technical language, with an executive summary at the beginning. The executive summary should be four or five concise paragraphs summarizing the process, analysis, gaps, risks, and recommendations. The remainder of the paper should cover details for the IT department, the risk management team, and the internal auditors.

Project plan creation

Creating a project plan to remediate the gaps and risks, using short, medium and long-term project milestones and tasks provides a path to achieving risk reduction. The plan should start with the highest risks and work through the list according to prioritization.

Identify resources

Identifying key project participants, and their tasks and time estimates is key in developing the project plan. Having clear ideas of what needs to be done and how to layer the tasks in with the existing project workload helps management to prioritize the remediation project against other business value-added projects already in the queue. It may be necessary to reach out to the different teams to get task estimates.

Future state architectural diagram and metrics

In preparing to communicate the project to upper management and key stakeholders, an architectural diagram of the future state should be drafted. This diagram is key to help show the before and after states of the risk management process, and to communicate the value of the project.

Create metrics for current risks, post-project risks, long-term risks and audit processes, and prepare a return on investment statement to execute the project. Upper management needs to understand why the project is important and what that risk reduction translates to in terms of long-term investment. The work does not end once the risks in the environment are remediated. There needs to be an ongoing plan to sustain the future state, and should include audit points to verify that new processes, such as security-note review and implementation, are occurring as promised.

Presentation of findings

Create a summary presentation for the assessment results to present to key stakeholders and leaders. This presentation takes the executive summary from the white paper and puts it into visual format. The critical points should be highlighted with visual representations, metrics and business impact statements.

5 Leveraging the NIST CIS Controls version 7.1 framework for SAP

Reconciling SAP cybersecurity to the NIST CIS Controls standardizes the analysis, risk management, and reporting processes for SAP. The benefit of using the NIST controls is that, in most cases, it enables a seamless integration of SAP into a company-wide, cyber risk management program.

5.1 Reconciling SAP Cybersecurity to the NIST CIS Controls

In order create a strong cybersecurity program, or to leverage an existing program for the benefit of securing the SAP Landscape, the first step is to understand the language used by security programs in general. One of the top road maps used to create a cybersecurity program is the NIST CIS Controls Version 7.1. The recommendations made by NIST are accepted worldwide as the most important in the information security industry and are considered industry standard.

The controls ask important questions about connectivity, users, vulnerability assessments, maintenance, defenses, services, disaster recovery, data protection and security, penetration testing, and incident response. It is appropriate to pose these questions against an entire IT infrastructure, but the same questions should also be drilled down into the application layer. This chapter will look at each of the controls and discuss how they apply to the application in the SAP landscape.

The controls are broken down into three levels: basic, foundational, and organizational. The basic controls are the guidelines to establish a base level of cyber hygiene:

Basic CIS Controls
1. Inventory and Control of Hardware Assets
2. Inventory and Control of Software Assets
3. Continuous Vulnerability Management

4. Controlled Use of Administrative Privileges

5. Secure Configuration for Hardware and Software on Mobile Devices, Laptops, Workstations and Servers

6. Maintenance, Monitoring and Analysis of Audit Logs

Foundational CIS Controls

7. Email and Web Browser Protections

8. Malware Defenses

9. Limitation and Control of Network Ports, Protocols and Services

10. Data Recovery Capabilities

11. Secure Configuration for Network Devices, such as Firewalls, Routers and Switches

12. Boundary Defense

13. Data Protection

14. Controlled Access Based on the Need to Know

15. Wireless Access Control

16. Account Monitoring and Control

Organizational CIS Controls

17. Implement a Security Awareness and Training Program

18. Application Software Security

19. Incident Response and Management

20. Penetration Tests and Red Team Exercises

Control 18 specifically addresses application software security. This applies to in-house or third-party software development and to the more standard, out-of-the-box software packages. It addresses software that does not require customization, internal or external communications, or application-level access management. SAP is much more complex than a standard application, containing its own communications, access management processes, and development language for custom internal applications. In order to understand how all the controls apply to this versatility, we will review each control in each level and discuss how these apply to SAP.

5.1.1   Basic CIS Controls

Control 1: Inventory and Control of Hardware Assets

Authorized devices should already be inventoried and properly secured but it is important to understand how unauthorized devices gain access to the SAP landscape. With the growth in the use of web-based access to SAP via portal, reporting, HANA, Fiori, and other HTTP-delivered content, as well as the growth of NetWeaver Business Client (NWBC), more types of devices can connect to the SAP environment. Bring-your-own-device policies that allow users to utilize personal computers and mobile devices for business use take control of the platform interacting with the SAP environment out of the hands of the IT department, and introduces new risk to the landscape. Hackers, using viruses, botnets, and worms may already have access to these unauthorized or unmanaged devices, and therefore also have the opportunity to drill down into the SAP data.

Control 2: Inventory and Control of Software Assets

Authorized software should go through a review, installation and maintenance process; but how does unauthorized software gain connectivity to the SAP landscape? All companies have a certain level of 'shadow IT', where business areas run IT projects in order to solve a business need. These projects can create connectivity to the SAP landscape for data augmentation, cloud-based access, remote access for consultants, and whatever software they implement, along with many other scenarios. Projects such as these provide external access to SAP, that goes through an RFC connection that may have very broad access. If the ID associated with the RFC connection has expansive access in the system, then the content of the system is at risk and the ability for malicious code to be injected into the server increases.

Controls 1 and 2 are inventories of devices and software on the network. Once you are aware of the authorized and unauthorized hardware and software on the network, steps need to be taken to harden the configurations of the authorized items and purge the unauthorized ones.

Control 3: Continuous Vulnerability Assessment

Continuous vulnerability assessment includes regular penetration testing, both internally in the corporate network, and externally. It also includes monitoring the network through a security information and event management (SIEM) tool for unauthorized access, excessive access/movement of data, management of breach attempts and forensic analysis.

Control 4: Controlled Use of Administrative Privileges

Some of the biggest security breaches in history occurred because of simple configuration changes that were overlooked. Changing the administrative ID and password that the hardware and software are delivered with is an action that is commonly missed. One of the first things to do when configuring a new item is to make a copy of the delivered administrative ID, together with all its access, and delete the delivered ID. Locking it, removing the password, and changing the password are all useful techniques; but if a hacker gains access through an ID that has lower access, but is able to change passwords or reactivate IDs, that administrative ID is now compromised. It is better to change the administrative ID to something easy to remember but innocuous, and store the password in an encrypted password tool located on a different server.

Securing the out-of-the-box administrative ID is critical, but it is also of great importance to make sure the systems and software administrators do not have too much access, that they change their passwords regularly, and that their access is suspended or terminated immediately upon leaving the company. These users often have large amounts of access across every on-premise and cloud application, so tracking and terminating this access everywhere is critical when they leave.

Your basis, security, development, and configuration team members should never have the SAP-delivered profiles SAP_ALL or SAP_NEW, or even an internally-created SAP_"almost". It is important to limit them to what they really require, and access to security transactions and tables should not be given to anyone outside of the security team. Leaving that open gives the administrative user the ability to add whatever access they want, including access to delete the history of what they have done directly from the tables.

Control 5: Secure Configurations for Hardware and Software

Secure configurations for both hardware and software requires that all vulnerabilities communicated by the manufacturer are applied as quickly as possible. There needs to be dedicated time for administrators to check the websites of the manufacturers of all hardware and software for the latest updates. This includes all software applications on the network.

SAP Notes for Security are security patches delivered by SAP. These need to be reviewed and applied in a timely manner. This is the process for managing vulnerabilities within SAP and is often overlooked. We will take a closer look at vulnerabilities in SAP in Chapter 6 and the SAP Security Notes process in Chapter 10.

Control 6: Maintenance, Monitoring, and Analysis of Audit Logs

There are two different types of configurable logs in SAP—the *system log* and the *security log*. The system log registers errors, warnings, and failed login attempts, and process messages are logged in the system log. Transaction SM21 accesses the system log.

The security audit log is turned off by default when the system is set up. It has specific parameters configured for it and can be set up to audit:

▶ Successful and unsuccessful dialog login attempts

▶ Successful and unsuccessful RFC logon attempts

▶ RFC calls to function modules

▶ Changes to the user master records

▶ Successful and unsuccessful transaction starts

▶ Changes to the audit configuration

To use the security audit log, the basis team needs to set it up by using the profile parameter information shown in Table 3.1.

Profile parameter	Definition	Standard or default value
rsau/enable	Activates the log on an application server	0 – Audit log is not turned on by default
rsau/local/file	File name and location for the log	/usr/sap/<SID>/<instno>/log/ audit_<SAP_instance_number>
rsau/max_diskspace_ local	Maximum size of audit log	1,000,000 bytes
rsau/selection_slots	Number of selec- tion slots for the audit	2

Table 5.1: Audit log profile parameters

You specify the activities that you want to log in filters using transaction SM19. You can read the log using transaction SM20. You can delete old logs with transaction SM18.

There are also table-level logs that record workflow, change documents, table changes, changes made via transport, and changes to the user and authorization information. For more information on available logs, see SAP Service Marketplace and search for Audit and Logging for the version and support pack of the system in question.

These logs should be reviewed regularly for anomalies and breach at-tempts. This sort of monitoring can be done via log-monitoring tools such as SAP Enterprise Threat Detection or SPLUNK.

The first four CIS controls work together fluidly as a process. First, you have to understand the devices connected to your network, what they are for, and how they got there—CSC Control 1. Next, you need to understand what software is on the network, who has access to it and what its purpose is—CSC Control 2. Once this inventory is in hand, secure configuration of both the hardware and software is necessary for data protection—CSC Control 3. Continuous monitoring of the network will alert of attempted breaches, unauthorized access, or high-volume data transferal in order to protect data from external intruders and internal mismanagement/fraud—CSC Control 4.

For detailed information on analyzing the Security Audit Log, refer to: *https://blogs.sap.com/2014/12/11/analysis-and-recommended-settings-of-the-security-audit-log-sm19-sm20/.*

See also Appendix A.

5.1.2   Foundational CIS Controls

Control 7: Email and Web Browser Protections

The use of NetWeaver Business Client (NWBC) and Fiori has made web-browser security extremely important. Both email and web-browser protections are customarily provided by the endpoint protection on the device, but there are numerous protocol and application security notes that impact the vulnerability of SAP when accessed through a web browser. The endpoint protection and security notes work together to protect the data. We will cover the specific threats to SAP in Chapter 6.

Control 8: Malware Defenses

SAP clients and application servers are subject to malware and ransomware attacks. The network intrusion prevention assists in preventing this, but all SAP Security Notes need to be implemented. The Solution Manager application, another module in the SAP Landscape, is able to determine what notes are missing and highlights the urgent and highest risk notes for these issues. We will be covering SAP Security Notes in depth in Chapter 10.

Control 9: Limitations and Control of Network Ports, Protocols and Services

One of the biggest holes in an SAP Security role design is the management of RFC authorization objects. The full list of transactions using RFC authorizations is available in transaction SU24 and in the USOBT table which contains the default transaction code for authorization assignment and configuration setups, or in the customized version of the same table—USOBT_C. These transactions break down into two categories: used by the end users and used for managing trusted relationships between systems/servers. The end user authorizations allow the execution of programs and retrieval of data from other servers or databases. The trusted relationships authorizations establish the connection between systems to enable the uninterrupted flow of data and program execution.

Getting RFC security under control

 Implementing new or improved control of RFC security will require a great deal of testing. Use security tracing to find the exact values to be filled into fields in the RFC authorization objects. This can be done with planned RFC testing, or during a full system regression test.

End users

End-user remote function call management is done at role level. The authorizations listed below are used to manage remote function call access and how it is controlled:

- ▶ *S_RFC*—Authorization Check for RFC Access. This is present and configurable in over 5,000 standard transactions and external services in ECC. This authorization object is controlled by:
  - ▶ *ACTVT*—Activity; option is Execute (16)
  - ▶ *RFC_TYPE*—RFC Type. Options for this field are Function Group (FUGR) and Function Module (FUNC). The necessary option is determined by the RFC program name and what it requires.
  - ▶ *RFC_NAME*—RFC Name. This is the program name that runs the RFC call. Historically, this was given an asterisk for global access, which is the core of the risk to the authorization. The program name can be determined by testing with tracing turned on. Most third-party transactions and programs have a list of program names delivered in the security guide.
- ▶ *S_RFC_ADM*—Administration for RFC Destination. Present and configurable in over 150 transactions, mostly used by the basis team for system configuration.
  - ▶ *ACTVT*—options are: create or generate (01), change (02), display (03), delete (06), and extend maintenance (36)
  - ▶ *ICF_VALUE*—Internet Communications Framework values
  - ▶ *RFCDEST*—Logical Destination (Specified in Function Call)
  - ▶ *RFCTYPE*—This is the type of system the RFC is connected to. Options include:

46

- ▶ Connection to R/2 System (2)
- ▶ Connection to ABAP System (3)
- ▶ HTTP Connection to External Server (G)
- ▶ HTTP Connection to ABAP System (H)
- ▶ Connection to Application Server with Same Database (I)
- ▶ Reference Entry (Refers to Other Destination) (L)
- ▶ CMC Connection (M)
- ▶ Start External Program Using SNA or APPC (S)
- ▶ Start External Program Using TCP/IP (T)
- ▶ RFC Using Special ABAP Driver Routines (X).
- ▶ *S_RFC_SHLP* – Authorization to use a search help via RFC. Search help to remote systems has to be configured by the basis team; it is not used by default.

Trusted server/system relationship

The trusted/trusting RFC destination relationship is setup by the basis team in transaction SM59. The relationship type is determined by the basis team during the system configuration. Errors in the trusted relationship can be viewed with transaction ST22. Any time the authorizations in the list below are in a role, that role should be evaluated for secure configuration of the fields and only granted if absolutely necessary:

- ▶ *S_RFC_TTAC*—Access Control for Trust relationships. Transaction SMTACL is used by the basis team to create trust relationships between systems.
- ▶ *S_RFC_TT*—Authorization object for Trusted-Trusting System Definition.
- ▶ *S_RFCACL*—Authorization Check for RFC User (e. g. Trusted System).
- ▶ *S_RFCRAIAR*—Authorization Object for RFC_ABAP_INSTALL_AND_RUN Function Module.

For more information, refer to the SAP Help Portal and search for "Trusted RFC: Authorization Objects" (the website at the time of writing is: *help.sap.com*).

Control 10: Data Recovery Capabilities

SAP is covered by the Business Continuity and Disaster Recovery Plan for most corporations. The backup and archiving of data is part of that plan, as are the processes for retrieving data from the backups.

Control 11: Secure Configuration for Network Devices, such as Firewalls, Routers, and Switches

Most of the network devices are external to SAP, but *SAProuter* is an SAP program that acts as a proxy in the network connectivity process between SAP Systems, and between SAP and external networks. SAProuter creates a firewall around the SAP systems, controlling the traffic coming in through the network firewall port directed to the SAP systems. This is a password-protected and encrypted connection that also helps to manage system performance. There are SAP Security notes issued for the SAProuter on a regular basis in order to patch vulnerabilities. In the process of prioritizing SAP note application, any notes for SAProuter should be given urgent priority for immediate application if at all possible.

For more information, refer to the SAP Help Portal and search for "SAProuter".

Control 12: Boundary Defense

The external network tools provide the bulk of the boundary defense. The rest is provided by SAProuter, as mentioned in Control 11.

Control 13: Data Protection

Data at rest, both in production and non-production environments, is an area of cybersecurity concern. Virtualization has increased and copying full data to testing and development environments has become common practice. This control addresses data security. In SAP, the key concerns are manufacturing master data, vendor masters, customer masters, and employee data. It is necessary to understand the risks to master data and to other critical data types in production, during a copyback, and in any non-production scenario.

Master data, risks to data, and tools and techniques to manage and protect data are covered in more detail in Chapter 13.

Control 14: Controlled Access Based on the Need to Know

Need-to-know access is a concept whereby users only get access to what they need in order to perform their job, and nothing else. This includes display access that is usually considered harmless. It is a strict principle of always limiting access. Controlling access based on the need to know is more complex than secure configuration. It requires business cooperation in ideals such as the principle of least privilege, data classification, secure onboarding and terminations, and user access reviews.

With the *principle of least privilege,* users are only granted access to exactly what they require and no more; this includes not allowing the access privileges of one user to be copied in order create or augment the access of another person.

With data classification, information is organized based on criticality. Data is labelled, and access to that data is managed appropriately; this includes decisions as to what information is available to everyone, what is restricted to certain business areas or management levels, and what is confidential information. Access roles can be designed around these classifications, or software can be purchased to flag the data by classification and to manage user access.

Control 15: Wireless Access Control

Except for the SAProuter, Wireless Access Control is managed through the network perimeter and mobile device policies/processes of the company. With the increasing use of Fiori, more wireless and mobile device access is necessary.

Control 16: Account Monitoring and Control

Secure onboarding and terminations ensure that when new user access is granted, it follows the principle of least privilege. This includes defined business processes for training new employees. A new employee may be very experienced in the job they are being hired for, but they should follow documented company processes, and should not try to introduce new processes (i.e., "I did this at my old job and I want to do it here"), requiring additional access without thorough vetting and approval. A secure terminations process includes the immediate removal of user access upon termination. A user's local PC files, email account, and network drive data can all be moved offline, out of the mainstream and production areas. This prevents access by the terminated employee, or collusion from someone else they know, to gather or remove information after they have left the company.

In a *user access review,* all access, for all users on the network, is reviewed in order to ensure users have only the access required. This also ensures that when a user has changed positions, their old access has been properly removed, and that no additional access has been granted to a user through other channels. This is a formal process requiring review and sign-off when completed.

Some additional key account monitoring actions include reviewing the SAP Logs to see what users are doing in the system. This can be done directly in the system, or in the SAP GRC Access Control product if the SAP landscape is connected to it; user execution data is stored there as well. You can monitor users who have many failed transaction executions or who attempt to access data in numeric order. Extremely long-running jobs kicked off by a user can be monitored as well. Users attempting to download large quantities of data can be a fraud or intellectual property theft concern. These processes can be automated using a program to review the data and which then send reports of excessive access attempts or long-running jobs to the user administrator or team.

5.1.3   Organizational CIS Controls

Control 17: Implement a Security Awareness and Training Program

Implementing a security awareness and training program for SAP depends on the access management process, role development processes, and how audits are performed. In general, there are several different categories of training:

▶ Security team training—this is internal to the security team and details the role creation, change, transport and retirement processes. It includes segregation of duties and security architectural model details.

▶ Business team training for security requirements—this is general training for business team members and for those who act as liaisons between security and the business, whether they are in the SAP Module functional configuration teams or in different business sectors. This training covers: how to submit new development or change requests to the development and security teams, what detailed information is needed, who the lead is on the request, who will use the solution in production, who will perform testing and how, any similarity to or inclusion of an SAP Standard transaction, what tables are being written to, and what the detailed level authorizations should be. This enables development and security teams to create a thoroughly secured and tested business solution and put that solution into the correct role for users to access.

▶ SAP program and interface developer training in security best practices and security implementation processes.

▶ Role change processes and approvals training.

▶ User administration processes and approvals training.

▶ Audit trail requirements and management training.

Control 18: Application Software Security

Application security has been broken down across a number of different controls. SAP has a *role-based access control* model. This means that access is built into roles that are assigned to users. As such, transactions and authorizations are placed in roles, and those roles are assigned to users. There are a couple of important, general rules for role development that cover all different security role architecture designs.

Transactions starting with the letter "S" are, in most cases, system administration transactions and should be limited in assignment to users.

Authorization objects starting with "S" are higher risk because they are system administration access transactions.

Changing standard transactions

 Standard transactions should not be modified. If a custom view or version of a standard SAP transaction is necessary, the custom transaction can be called with a variant, or copied to a custom transaction, and the changes made to the custom version. Changes made to standard transactions could contain insecure code hiding risk and can be overwritten during upgrades.

When custom transactions are being created, they need to be programmed to be authorization relevant. This means that the custom code calls out to authorization objects so they can be secured by activity, group, table, or other key authorization fields. By calling out to the authorization object, the update of this custom code happens every time the authorizations are upgraded by SAP. If the authorization code is incorporated or copied into the custom transaction, it cannot be secured at field level and can be a security and cybersecurity risk.

Role and transaction changes should not be made in production. All changes should be transported from the development environment. This is from both a system-risk and a change-management perspective. On the risk side, the production system should not be open for development because this also means it is open to hackers. From the change management perspective, if changes are made somewhere other than the development environment, the risk of losing the change due to overwrite is very high.

Third-party software should be installed in a sandbox system, outside of the production transport path, and tested before being implemented in the transport path. If there are consultants doing the installation, they should provide the basis and security teams with the installation and security guides for the system, and prepare roles for the project. This should include information regarding tables, RFC, authorization objects, role development, and transactions. The security team should provide a design-guidance document to the third-party installers, which contains the security guidelines for how access is secured and given to users.

Control 19: Incident Response and Management

Incident response and management works a little differently within SAP than in other applications. User access management is still managed the same way, but the transport process requirement changes any immediate response to emergency issues. There should be written procedures for incident-response processes in order to manage SAP-related emergency change management.

Having an elevated access management process for emergency issue resolution in the production environment allows for rapid response for things that are not transportable. Tools such as SAP GRC Emergency Access Management allow for elevated access in production systems for emergency responses. For any emergency access management tool or process there also needs to be an approval and logging process. The emergency access logs need to be reviewed as soon as possible and signed off by the process owner or manager. The log review process confirms the requirement of the emergency fix, that nothing else was done with that elevated access, and that a record of the tasks performed, reviewed, and signed off are saved for review by auditors.

Control 20: Penetration Tests and Red Team Exercises

Penetration tests and red team exercises are activities where one or more people, or software, deliberately test the network setup to try and penetrate the systems. These can be done from inside or outside the network. There are penetration test tools that are specifically for SAP. They use code transported into the SAP system and then perform a test from within, or external to, the network. They can also do penetration tests without importing any transports into SAP. It depends on what type of test is in scope and what different vendors have to offer.

Detailed knowledge of SAP Security enables the system to be made compliant within the NIST CIS Control Framework. The details of this chapter create a path for making SAP compliant with the framework. It also sets up the system for future compliance within the CMMC Framework for US Government Suppliers. In the CMMC Model Appendices, there is a source mapping appendix that maps other security frameworks to the CMMC domains. This is very helpful to start the maturity process required to achieve, or maintain, the status of US government supplier.

For more information about the CMMC and to find the appendices, refer to: *https://www.acq.osd.mil/cmmc/.*

6 Cybersecurity threats to SAP

The threat matrix for SAP is much the same as any network or web application. Historically, however, SAP has not been managed as though there were threat actors intent on infiltrating the application and databases. This has left SAP playing catch-up in terms of risk management that is not related to segregations of duties and financial fraud. The threat matrix for SAP includes historic threats, integration threats and hackers.

6.1 Historic threats—users, customization, no post-go-live cleanup, no archiving

6.1.1 Users

Historically, SAP lived inside the perimeter of the firewall (see Figure 6.1). It enjoyed protection provided by firewalls and intrusion-prevention tools maintained by network security administrators, as well as old-fashioned security through obscurity.

SAP Security focused on things internal to the system and on securing what users could do.

Historic Threat	Integration	Hackers
Users		
Access	AaaS	
Customization	SaaS	Vulnerabilities
Cleanup	IaaS	Code Injection
Archiving	Portal	DDOS
	Mobile	Data Breach

Figure 6.1: Threat matrix

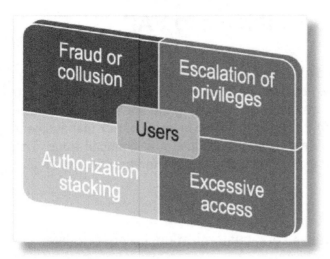

Figure 6.2: User-level risks

Users have always been the greatest risk to a system (see Figure 6.2). From simple errors to mass updates that were incorrect, it is a historical fact that there will always be a need for functional experts with escalated privileges to undo accidents. The deeper level issues come when there is intent to bring harm to the system or to defraud the company. This could be a planned activity, or a situation where a user discovers they can access something they previously did not know about and find ways to use that to their benefit. User-level risks are:

▶ Fraud or collusion

▶ Escalation of privileges in roles

▶ Authorization stacking

▶ Excessive access

Requirements for separation of duties have made fraud or collusion risks well known in the security design process. When role specifications are developed and tested for separation of duties risks for the production environment, the risk is lowered, but the problem persists in quality assurance and testing environments. When elevated access is provided for testers working with a copy of the production data, users are able to find things they shouldn't, or can download data that could be used for fraud. Data-masking and carefully considering what elevated access users need on production copies can mitigate this risk.

Escalation of privileges in roles occurs in several different scenarios. The lowest risk is found in roles created using the default authorizations. These are pulled in with the transactions and require the population of empty fields. The way in which these fields are populated is where the risk can be introduced. Keeping the access granted in these fields targeted, with as few stars as possible (a star * grants unlimited access) is best practice to minimize risk. When these fields are filled in with stars, or if the default field values are changed, the risk is increased because users can see and manipulate more information than necessary. The highest escalation of privilege risks in roles are introduced when authorization objects are entered in roles manually, instead of being bound by the transaction to default authorizations. Authorizations entered in this fashion have no boundaries on the field settings, and when transactions are removed from a role, the manually entered authorizations remain. The remaining and orphaned authorizations impact all the other transactions in the roles, as well as all roles assigned to the user.

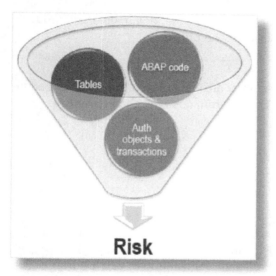

Figure 6.3: Authorization stacking risk

Authorization stacking is when all the transactions and authorizations assigned to a user through their roles are combined, thereby increasing what actions users have access to in the system (see Figure 6.3). These accumulate in the user buffer and, unless specifically programmed otherwise, the field values in authorizations combine and increase the overall access to that authorization as it is represented in the buffer. This can change a display transaction to provide all the create or change functionality without actually having the create or change transaction. It also results in buttons and menu options being available that wouldn't be otherwise.

Excessive access, due to roles that are no longer needed, includes being overprovisioned for a job, retaining access from a previous or different job, or tasking changes not being removed from a user's profile. Recent studies have shown that, on average, users only execute 7%-13% of the authorization they have been granted. This level of overprovisioning is a very high risk in SAP. Regular user access reviews remove this risk.

User access reviews

 Regular user access reviews are the best line of defense against overprovisioning. They can be cumbersome and time consuming in large organizations. Breaking them up by region or functional area and doing different groups quarterly can streamline the process.

Customizations create risk when they are not created to be authorization-relevant or are left unsecured. The different customization types are:

- ▶ Custom ABAP code
- ▶ Authorization objects
- ▶ Transactions
- ▶ Tables

Custom ABAP code is a risk when it is programmed not to call out to authorization objects, but instead pulls all the authorization object code into itself. If the code is written to be authorization relevant, then when a transaction is created for it, that transaction can be added to the user defaults table, USOBT_C, that is maintained with transaction SU24. When the transaction is added in SU24, the relationships to authorization objects are added with the default values that are needed. When those transactions are added to roles, all necessary authorizations are pulled in automatically. The same process is done for custom transactions and authorization objects. They need to be associated in SU24 so that they are added by default and follow best practices for security. Custom tables need to be categorized into a custom table authorization group. Leaving it blank either excludes it from being accessed by roles, or puts it in with other tables that have no association with the customizations being secured. Creating custom table (Z*) authorization groups is the best way to secure custom tables. Common practice is to have a Z table authorization group by module (e. g., ZFI, ZMM, etc.).

6.1.2 Post-project cleanup

Most teams are so laden with new project work that cleaning up after a new project goes live is not a priority. This can leave access open, objects and code orphaned, and can leave other items in the landscape that could be utilized for nefarious purposes.

6.1.3 Archiving

Archiving is another housekeeping item that often falls by the wayside. Old and unnecessary data left in the system exposes employees, customers, vendors, and intellectual property to risk of exposure.

6.2 The new and emerging threat matrix for SAP

6.2.1 Integration risks

SAP was originally designed to be a privately hosted software, housed in a datacenter, with little access to the outside world. The architecture has been updated to manage external connectivity, and is constantly being improved to better secure the datatypes that hackers specifically search for. Integration of SAP into cloud-based applications and services increases SAP's *attack surface*—the sum of the different points where an unauthorized user can get access to the network.

Cloud integration includes services such as:

- ▶ Infrastructure as a Service (IaaS)
- ▶ Software as a Service (SaaS)
- ▶ Platform as a Service (PaaS)
- ▶ Identity as a Service (IDaaS)
- ▶ Security as a Service (SECaaS)

It is important to understand the risks to the environment which can be introduced by externally hosted (cloud) services. Risks are introduced into the environment any time you have cloud applications integrated with internally managed SAP, externally hosted data centers housing entire SAP landscapes, externally hosted SAP instances, production or non-production, or any connection to any data not located in your own datacenter that is used to enhance SAP Data. These integration points and external systems are attack surfaces used by hackers to enter into your network and systems. Each one of these cloud services, systems, and datastores have their own risks. A hacker can break into any of these points and use that connection to penetrate the network and systems hosted internally. For each connection and service, there is a responsibility to perform a vulnerability assessment to ensure that all parties perform the proper due diligence in securing their systems. When using software or PaaS, a certain amount of risk is transferred to the provider. This is helpful on paper, but there is always an impact once the data is compromised; and that impact falls on all parties involved. Once intellectual property, trade secrets and the PII of a company is compromised, recovery is a long and difficult process.

6.2.2 Mobile devices and bring-your-own-device (BYOD)

Mobile devices, whether company-owned or employee-owned, which are being used for company tasks (company email, applications, etc.) are all at risk. The risks include: loss of device, data transmission security, application security, data storage, external breach at the service provider's location, and unauthorized access by users employed by the service provider. Mobile device management software can protect against this by encrypting the device, *compartmentalizing* company data (separating it from personal data and applications), and creating the ability to wipe the entire device remotely if it is lost or stolen.

Mobile access introduces risks for penetration, data theft, or data manipulation into the environment via:

- ▶ Mobility gateways
- ▶ Fiori
- ▶ SAP applications utilizing mobile access
- ▶ Externally created SAP modules utilizing mobile access
- ▶ Barcode scanners

▶ Email approvals

▶ Excel workbooks accessed from a mobile device with links to SAP or BI data

6.2.3 Cloud risks

Cloud security risks are the same as the risks in a datacenter, with the following additions:

▶ Interfaces and application programming interfaces (APIs) associated with the cloud service are used to enhance or maintain data or to create pathways into the system for hackers.

▶ The virtual machine environment and database sharing have the risk of cross contamination from virus and worms as well as data being exposed in shared environments.

▶ The shared location means that your neighbor's data breach could also be yours if it exploits vulnerabilities down at system level.

Who owns the risk

 Understanding where the responsibility and accountability lies for security and vulnerability management is key to securing operations that use cloud services.

6.3 Hackers—the most common threats and abuses

Why do hackers want your systems and what they are after in SAP? Hackers use system and access vulnerabilities to breach systems, steal information, infect systems, and launch attacks on other systems both internally and externally.

Threat actors look to break into the database or manipulate the SAP system directly. In both cases, they are looking to harvest data for their own financial benefit. This could be directly, by changing bank account data to redirect deposits, or more indirectly, by looking for information they can sell. That information includes names, addresses, social security numbers or other personally identifiable financial information, credit card data, bank account data, etc. They also search for intellectual property that can be sold to competitors or on foreign markets.

The following sections outline the abuses that can create the greatest threats in SAP.

6.3.1 Cross-site scripting

With *cross-site scripting (XSS),* attackers insert a program or script into web pages that are accessed by other users. XSS vulnerability allows attackers to bypass credentials and access controls. In general, cross-site scripting refers to the hacking technique that leverages vulnerabilities in the code of a web application to allow an attacker to send malicious content from an end user and collect some type of data from the victim.

6.3.2 Missing authorization checks

Missing authorization checks in code can enable an authenticated attacker to abuse functionality and leverage privileges in the system, and access data that should be restricted.

6.3.3 Directory traversal

A *directory traversal* (or path traversal) is a vulnerability where attackers bypass security or there is no security validation to stop hackers from moving through directory trees on the server. This allows hackers to exploit insufficient security validation to access restricted directories and run commands external to the web server's root directory. The goal of this attack is to order an application to access a computer file that is not intended to be accessible. This attack exploits a lack of security built into the application, even though the software is acting exactly as it is supposed to, as opposed to exploiting a bug in the code. Directory traversal can enable the attacker to gain access to the server's root password file, thus compromising administrative and user access. The attacker can then use the user IDs and passwords to log into the server and obtain information.

6.3.4   SQL injection

An *SQL injection* attack consists of the insertion or "injection" of an SQL query via the input data from the client to the application. A successful SQL injection can read sensitive data from the database, modify database data (insert/update/delete), execute administration operations on the database (such as shut down the database management system (DBMS)), recover the content of a given file present on the DBMS file system, and in some cases, issue commands to the operating system.

6.3.5   Information disclosure

Information disclosure vulnerability is where system data or debugging information is revealed, thereby helping an adversary to learn about the system and form a plan of attack. An information leak occurs when system data or debugging information leaves the program through an output stream or logging function. Basically, leaving a program in debug mode, or having debug access on users in a production environment, places the system at risk for this type of vulnerability.

6.3.6   Code injection

With *code injections,* attackers inject code into a program that is then executed by the application. This type of attack exploits poor handling of untrusted data. These types of attacks are usually possible due to a lack of proper input/output data validation, for things such as: allowed characters (standard regular expressions classes or custom), data format, and the amount of expected data.

Code injection differs from *command injection* in that an attacker is only limited by the functionality of the injected language. This can include the injection of malware and viruses into the application or server.

6.3.7 Authentication bypass

While most applications require authentication to gain access to private information or to execute tasks, not every authentication method is able to provide adequate security. In the case of *authentication bypass,* authentication schemes are bypassed by simply skipping the log-in page and directly calling an internal page that is supposed to be accessed only after authentication has been performed. This could be due to negligence, ignorance, or a simple underestimation of security threats. In addition, it is often possible to bypass authentication measures by tampering with requests and tricking the application into thinking that the user is already authenticated. This can be accomplished either by modifying the given URL parameter, by manipulating the form, or by counterfeiting sessions.

6.3.8 Hardcoded credentials

With *hardcoded credentials,* a user ID and password is hard-coded into the application, web page, or URL and an attacker can locate these credentials and use them to access the affected system.

6.3.9 Verb tampering

Verb tampering, also known as HTTP tampering, utilizes web programming and database SQL language verbs such as GET, POST or HEAD to gain access to restricted information. This is used in conjunction with an XSS attack.

6.3.10 HANA

As a large-scale, in-memory database, HANA is vulnerable to SQL injection attacks, verb tampering attacks, command and control attacks. If HANA is compromised, there is a higher risk to the company than a standalone SAP server because all data is live. With more data in memory than a standard SAP implementation, there is little or no data at rest with the ability to secure and obfuscate.

6.3.11 Mobile device

Mobile devices pose several risks to corporate resources. The vulnerabilities previously discussed can be utilized via malware on a mobile device. Unbeknownst to an employee, they might download malware-infected or malicious applications, thereby giving third parties access to data and connections. The employee might think they are being cautious about OS updates on their device, or that they are downloading an innocuous game from the app store, but these actions can result in data loss or breach without even being aware what is happening.

Other risks from mobile device usage include: hacking through the use of unsecured or free WIFI connections, lost or stolen devices, data-management issues (i.e., no segregation of data between personal and corporate information), and disgruntled (or former) employees with company data on personal devices.

6.3.12 Fiori

The risks to SAP Fiori are the same as for any mobile device and can be found in any bring-your-own-device (BYOD) program. Web security risks, including cross-site scripting and device-based malware, are all risks to the SAP landscape when content is delivered through the mobile communications channels with Fiori access.

It is the responsibility of the SAP Security, basis, network, and cybersecurity teams to manage of these risks and threats. Input from all parties is required in order to close gaps and quickly remediate new zero-day vulnerabilities.

7 Implementing cybersecurity risk management in SAP

Implementing a cybersecurity risk management program in SAP starts by changing the mindset regarding what SAP Security encompasses. Managing cyber risk in SAP expands the role of the SAP security team to include security auditing of tasks in the basis team's area, as well as architectural details.

7.1 Managing the new, combined level of risk

In light of our changing world, we need to take a different view of security; one that looks at the outside world, and how data comes and goes from the internet, all the way down to the operating system and back.

What does 'basis' contain

SAP responsibility areas start with the SAP systems administration team, also known as the basis team. Basis is a formal responsibility area in SAP. All software installation fall under the basis title and is managed by the basis administrators. Basis level risks are the most common and highest vulnerability.

Managing the threat matrix starts by understanding the "basis" level risks and implementing a monthly or quarterly program for:

▶ Database patching

▶ Operating system patching

▶ Reviewing all connections touching data outside of SAP to ensure they are fully secured according to the most current recommendations from SAP

▶ User access reviews and password policies

▶ Security note applications

7.2 Connections, users, security notes, and SAP penetration testing

The first step in implementing cybersecurity is to know your connections. You need to be aware of where data comes from, where it goes, and how it is transmitted. It is necessary to secure your RFC connections by program name at all times; not just for dialogue users, but for all background users. The SAP Router, SAP Message Server, SAP Microsoft Management Console, SAP Dispatcher, and SAP HostControl all need to be secured; and you should review and apply all SAP Notes for these areas, as well as all SAP Security Notes.

The importance of user security continues to be a very high priority, but it is not just about dialogue users and what they can do. System, service, and communication users are at risk from internal and external threats, even if they cannot be directly logged in. There are some basic principles and processes that can increase system security without a large financial investment.

First, you can pretend that *SAP_ALL* and *SAP_NEW* do not exist, especially for service and system IDs. Hackers can break into a system using system, service, and communications users, and then use them to access data and escalate permissions. These attacks are harder to diagnose and link back to the hacker.

You can also perform regular user access reviews based on transaction usage and remove all access that is not being actively used.

In addition, you should set a requirement for users to implement complex passwords and regularly change the passwords.

A further process that can increase security is to implement role approvals and be sure the people approving the access are in the same location or department as the person being given the access. A user's manager should be the first line of approval for any new access request. Someone from corporate should not be approving access for someone on the other side of the world. The role approvers should know who they are giving the access to instead of providing blanket approvals.

7.3   Leverage SAP Access Control to manage risk

The tools and workflows in GRC Access Control enable you to manage risk in several ways. You can perform user access reviews and identify trans-actions that are not being used by users or groups; and then target them for removal. In addition, you are able to manage critical business and IT functions through the EAM (Emergency Access Management) capability.

7.4   Security role rebuild

A further way to increase system security, is to consider a security role rebuild. This enables you to create a task-based role environment based on historic transaction usage, assign transactions to one role suite only, and create a derived role environment for easy identification and assignment. Additionally, you can implement simple role names and the ability to assign them in a granular fashion. A security role rebuild is also useful to reduce access and authorization stacking, and improve reporting.

7.5   SAP Security Notes

Apply SAP Security Notes on a regular basis, and as often as the business and project work cycle permits, paying special attention to the SAP Secu-rity News page, located at: *https://support.sap.com/kb-incidents/notifications/ security-notes.html.*

Security notes are critical to prevent the latest known hacks, and to repair any vulnerabilities found during development and testing, or which are iden-tified by SAP customers. We will cover the SAP Security Notes process in depth in Chapter 10.

7.6   Cloud vendor review, mobile device policy and management

In conjunction with your network security and legal groups, you need to per-form a regular review of all cloud services and vendors that have any connectivity to the SAP landscape. Request a current SOC 2 audit document for system security from all vendors, and ensure they are compliant with best security practices. Insist that any cloud applications and vendors connecting to your systems have a SOC 2 report that can be reviewed prior to signing a contract. Audit reports that are required for a cloud security review include one or more of the following: SOC 1, SOC 2, SOC 3, and SSAE 16.

BYOD risks are numerous, such as: loss of a device containing proprietary data, recycling devices that are not properly wiped, disgruntled or terminated employees accessing and abusing company data. Risks at the technical level still exist in the form of toxic user applications, applications with cyber vulnerabilities, and applications stealing or leaking data. There are device vulnerabilities, device-based malware, data theft over public networks, application vulnerabilities, and theft through apps.

There are several ways to mitigate these risk, the simplest one being: do not allow personal devices to be on the company network!

If a company allows personal devices to be used to receive business emails, connect to the network, access company data, and connect to company applications, then a *mobile device management (MDM)* software suite is the solution.

An MDM suite installs a firewall on the device, encrypts communication, and creates an encrypted container where corporate data is stored. It has a remote wipe feature allowing the administrator to wipe all data from the entire phone, or only from the encrypted container, if the device is lost or stolen, or if an employee is terminated.

7.7   Tools to monitor compliance

There are many tools on the market to monitor, detect, and prevent risk within the enterprise and in SAP. The SAP GRC toolset can be leveraged to monitor high-risk access via Access Control. Consider creating a custom rulebook to track audit and cyber risks. Manage emergency or elevated access via Access Control EAM tools. Set up automated and manual controls in SAP Process Control. Process Control can be used to monitor system patching, security notes, and versioning, by creating controls connected to SAP Solution Manager reports.

7.7.1 SAP penetration testing

Perform SAP penetration testing from both internal and external locations. A *penetration test* assesses the security of the configuration of the basis-level components such as SAP Router, the proliferation of SAP_ALL, database-level security, and operating system-level security. There are a number of good tools on the market to perform this testing either as a service or with licensed ownership of the tool.

7.7.2 Mobile device policy

Implement a mobile device policy and a BYOD policy. The policy needs to define what types of devices can access the corporate network and what they can be used for, and should also inform the user of the device that the company has the right to wipe the device whenever the need arises.

7.7.3 Mobile device management software

A mobile device management solution places *antivirus* and *antimalware* software or a monitoring function on the device. This monitors the device's traffic, looking for anomalies and high data volumes that are out of the normal use patterns for the user. The software creates secure and encrypted data containers on the device to store and segregate company data, and enables remote location access in order to wipe the device should it be lost or stolen, or if the employee leaves the company.

7.7.4 SAP Enterprise Threat Detection

SAP Enterprise Threat Detection uses SAP HANA to connect SAP and non-SAP systems in order to manage social engineering risks, breach detection, fraud, employee-created breaches, and password abuse.

7.7.5 Other SAP tools

Additional products and solutions include:

▶ *User Interface Logging*—monitors user keystrokes

▶ *Field Masking*—masks fields to obfuscate or entirely hide fields from users

▶ *EarlyWatch Alerts*—security reports created by SAP Solution Manager

▶ *Code Vulnerability Analysis*—a code analysis tool for ABAP

Understanding the risks is the first step to managing the risks in SAP. Using information on the specific vulnerabilities and the methods for remediating or monitoring those risks creates the foundation for a vulnerability analysis of SAP. This analysis feeds into the creation of a case to implement a remediation plan, and the return on investment of doing so.

8 Policy and education

In this chapter, we will take a high-level look at the types of documentation and education necessary for a successful cybersecurity program. Understanding these items at a high level helps the SAP team to understand where their responsibilities fit in the cybersecurity program and how to communicate that to members of upper management, information technology, and the business.

8.1 Security policy, standards and procedures

The primary documents required in a cybersecurity program are: policies, standards, audit controls, procedures, and guidelines (see Figure 8.1) With the exception of guidelines, all these documents are required and compliance is measured against them. Guidelines are not required and are usually system, technology stack, or application-specific. They are the best practice ideals that can help to define the standards documents.

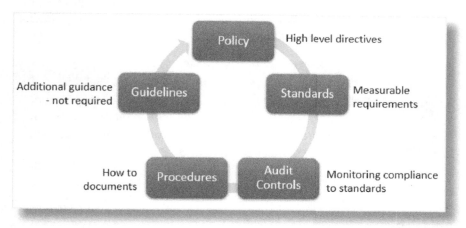

Figure 8.1: Policy and procedure documents

Policy and education is the most important, and most difficult, step in a cybersecurity program. Policy sounds easy but it is not as simple as writing up a document that says "no downloading unknown attachments or visiting web sites not related to business". First, downloading attachments and visiting web sites needs to be very clearly defined, and the wording needs to be carefully reviewed by the legal department. Once approved by legal, it also needs to be approved by HR and the Board of directors. When there is a fully approved policy, decisions need to be made about how to enforce and monitor it and what the incentives are for employees to comply. This process can take months and after it is completed, it needs to be socialized and an education program developed.

The education program needs to be aimed at the different levels of employees' responsibilities, and employees need to formally sign off to confirm they understand. Once a formal education process is in place, there needs to be a *security awareness program* that continually reminds employees of their responsibilities. An awareness program can include things such as stickers on computers reminding users not to share passwords, or customizations to the SAP logon screen to remind users that there is an audit-logging process that records their actions.

This level of formality is necessary because corporate policy is legally enforceable by the corporation, and there can also be legal consequences against the corporation. For example, if a hacked company had a corporate systems patching policy that stated they must patch all servers with the latest patching within one month of the release of the patch, and their employees were weeks or months behind, there could be a greater civil penalty against that company. The company in turn could then pursue litigation against the employees that did not comply.

Existing policy and security awareness program

 Policy and education would fall under an existing security policy and security awareness education program if one exists. Integrating into that program will increase awareness and priority of business critical SAP data.

8.1.1 Policy

The key to simplifying policy management and keeping corporate policy up-to-date with the rate of change in technology is to have a policy that is generic and high-level. A policy should consist of directive language, with phrases such as: "hard drives will be encrypted to the latest encryption standard" and "employees will not share their assigned logon information".

Security policies should be written according to the following:

▶ The policy should be enforceable and flexible.

▶ The policy should be simple and stated in a way that all audiences can understand it and why it exists.

▶ The policy should be written from a high-level directive perspective. Details on how these are implemented are kept in the reference procedure and standards documents that are constantly being maintained.

▶ The policy should reflect a best-case scenario, but should also relate to the reality of the corporate culture.

▶ The policy should be measurable.

▶ The policy should minimize unintended consequences.

▶ The policy should be reviewed annually, or whenever there are major corporate or technological changes.

The policy refers to specific process documents, which enable it to point to other, smaller process documents. These process documents are individually updated—annually and as required—to match the rate of technological evolution. The same review process is carried out, but is done by the management team, and is not as rigorous or critical as a formal policy review.

A framework is put in place to define the process topic, procedures, communication, education, ownership, sign-off, review and renewal, and audit processes. This framework makes updates and change communication regarding process and procedures documents a repeatable process, at a more granular level.

8.1.2 Standards

Standards documents are formal requirements regarding processes, actions, and configurations. Standards apply to hardware configurations, software configurations, access management processes, and all other aspects within information technology. The purpose of standards documents is to maintain a baseline of what the output should be for consistency and reliability. When technology or processes are changed, the standards documents are updated to reflect those changes. The standards documents are also used to audit IT processes for compliance.

8.1.3 Audit controls

Audit controls are documents used to test that standards and procedures are being followed, especially regarding actions that create risk. Audit controls are part of the annual financial audit for publicly traded companies, but that is only a fraction of what they are used for. Audit control documents are instructions on how to test compliance to each standard and procedure. These documents include information on what kind of sample data is necessary for testing, where to get the sample, what to review, and how to report the findings of the audit.

8.1.4 Procedures

Procedures are step-by-step instructions on how to perform a task, such as imaging a laptop or performing user-access management. For every task, there should be a procedure document. It is a significant amount of documentation once all the necessary steps are outlined, but the benefits in standardization, training new hires, and ensuring standards and audit requirements are met, outweigh the time spent creating and maintaining the documents. Whenever there is a process or technological change, the procedures documents should be validated to make sure each step is still applicable, and a review date and reason for the review should be added to the document. The procedures documents are the first thing to check if there are problems with the audit control findings. If the audit controls test according to the standards, and the procedures have not been updated with any process changes that came out of changes to the standards, it will lead to negative findings in the audit. Users need to be informed whenever changes are made to the procedures documents to ensure that actions are changed according to the new task definitions.

8.1.5 Guidelines

Guidelines are best-practice documents provided for the different applications. There are best-practice documents for software and hardware configuration, installation, and maintenance. SAP teams are familiar with the SAP Best Practice guides, and also know the best way to do things in a perfect world. The benefit is that guidelines provide a plan and a path for making improvements. Guideline documents are not mandatory in a security program and they are not subject to any review by audit.

8.2 Applying policy to SAP

8.2.1 Education

While education at the cybersecurity program level is not under the ownership of SAP Application Security, there are contributions to be made at the SAP level. There are some procedure documents that the SAP Security and basis teams can create that improve the overall result for all SAP users. The SAP teams may need to contribute audit documents on controls for GRC/user access management. These documents, once socialized to the IT departments and business, help guide change moving forward.

8.2.2 SAP security standards and practices

Having a set of security standards creates a fully informed work process between the project development teams and the security team. Without detailed instructions on how to interact with the SAP Security team and when, security is often an afterthought in the project development process. The following are examples of what a standards and practices document contains:

▶ No development work will be done in any system without a project and specification, or a help desk ticket. All work must be fully documented for audit purposes.

▶ No one is allowed to have SAP_ALL, SAP_NEW or SAP_'ALMOST' in any system in any landscape unless it is an emergency repair and a system is either down or about to be down.

▶ Only the SAP Security team or its assigned consultants may have SU01, PFCG, SU10, SU24, SU25, SU02 in any quality assurance or production system.

▶ Only the SAP Security team or its assigned consultants may create users, modify users (with the exception of password changes), delete users, create roles, modify roles, assign roles, delete roles, or transport roles.

▶ All SAP standard roles (starting with SAP_*) must be copied to a new name to be assigned and used in the system. No SAP standard role may be used or modified.

▶ All development is done in the development system and transported through to production. To do anything else means roles will not be the same in the entire landscape and changes can be overwritten when transports are implemented.

▶ All new custom transactions and authorization objects must be coded to be authorization relevant. This means that the authorization object code is not replicated inside the new program, but instead, the new program calls out to the authorization object. This is standard process for SAP Standard transactions and allows the security team to control what objects are needed for each custom transaction and how they perform in the system.

▶ All custom programs and tables must be in custom name space authorization groups. Custom transactions and programs assigned to transactions need to be assigned to the appropriate development class for classification and maintenance during upgrades and support-pack applications.

▶ When creating standard roles there will be no manually entered authorizations in the roles profile or changed authorizations. All authorization objects should be in a status of standard or maintained in the role's profile. Authorizations that are entered and changed manually cannot be tracked back to determine why they were set up that way or what transaction and change request made this happen. These are security holes and will not upgrade properly or respond to the application of security notes and vulnerability resolutions.

▶ When creating a new landscape, the transport path rules must also be followed, regardless of the production status of the future production server. No development can be done in that production server, regardless of its non-production status. Once it becomes a production server, its logs are subject to all audit requirements and will cause the audit to fail, regardless of when those changes took place.

▶ No transports will be moved without complete documentation, including test results; to do so will cause the company to fail the annual audit.

▶ When reporting an issue, the SAP Security team requires the following information:

　　▶ Transaction Code, system, user ID, and data entered into the fields of the transaction for reproducing the issue

- ▶ Precise fields with screen shots
- ▶ SU53 error reports with a full screenshot of the error report— enter */nSU53* in the transaction window after the error is received. Click through any pop-up windows generated during the error and generate the error report.

This set of standards is not an exhaustive list of the kinds of information that project teams need in order to understand what the SAP Security team requires for maintaining the environment. Most project teams do not understand the ramifications of their custom code during a support pack application or upgrade. Engaging in this manner creates an opportunity for dialogue and earlier integration of security design in the project.

8.2.3 Change management procedures

Clear change management, testing and transport procedures are important to the overall maintenance of a secure and stable SAP landscape. Basis teams often encounter issues with transport orders, overwrites, and getting all the correct transports moved for a project. There are several very good transport management software applications on the market, but a good change management process can work just as well as a software tool.

Part of the change management process is standardizing and publishing testing procedures. These same procedures work for multiple stages of testing and a clear set of testing procedures helps all parties involved in a project to manage their duties. The following section provides an example of a security-role testing procedure.

Security-role testing procedures (acceptance testing)

A baseline set of role testing procedures set expectations for testing and the promotion of roles to production. An example of a basic set of testing procedures is as follows:

- ▶ Assumptions—security roles will be tested during acceptance testing; all parent and child roles will be tested.
- ▶ Procedure:
  - ▶ Security administration will set up acceptance test users in the test environment, with the proper roles.

- ► Acceptance testers must report any problems encountered, that are suspected to be caused by security authorizations, to the project team role owner.
- ► If the problem is security related, the security role owners/testers must document the problem by running transaction SU53. They need to note the transaction code involved as well as any other information that may be helpful.
- ► The security role owner will notify the security admin team member assigned to the project.
- ► The security administration team must resolve the problem as quickly as possible.

From the assumptions point above, a *parent role* is the set of SAP transactions that can be performed by a person in a particular position. A *child role* is derived from the parent, and therefore contains all the same transactions. It contains specific organizational values that define authority for a given business unit, plant, sales org, etc.

From two examples outlined above, it is easy to see how procedures documents in the SAP environment fit into the overall cybersecurity program document repository. When the procedures are followed for role testing, the process of managing the change into production is clean and easily communicated. These procedures hit on some of the key audit controls around software development, testing and change management. Lack of documentation for these areas in SAP can trigger an audit failure.

9 Governance, risk, and compliance

Governance, risk and compliance is an end-to-end process to perform risk assessments, implement and maintain security controls, and perform security audits. This process ensures that the security improvements made are maintained and any new risks are managed in a timely fashion.

9.1 Overview

Governance, risk, and compliance is not strictly the SAP module. It is a standard set of processes, policies and procedures used to manage risk across an entire business. This risk relates to potential financial loss to the company. By measuring, monitoring, and mitigating risk, the company is able to control the potential financial loss.

In most cases, analysis and reporting of financial risk is done by internal and/or external auditors. The measurement of risk is done by reviewing the published procedures and measuring compliance to those procedures. This is done by taking a sample of changes made in the system and reviewing all the documentation, audit trails, and change histories to determine if the procedures were followed and documented, and that proper approval was acquired. Documentation must be provided explaining the circumstances around each change found that does not follow the documented procedures. If there is no documentation or approval indicating why the process was not followed, this is considered an audit finding and is reported to upper management as an increased risk to the system. All the different risks found are categorized and analyzed for their potential impact, and their risk is measured. Categories of risk include: potential financial loss due to fraud, system security vulnerability, data loss potential, system instability, and loss of productivity. For example, if a change is introduced into the system and is found to have caused a corruption of a critical financial table which then had to be rolled back, this falls into the categories of system instability, loss of productivity and data loss. If this change is found to have not followed the change management, testing and sign-off procedures, and is not fully documented, it is an audit finding and is reported to senior management.

In the previous chapter, we discussed specific procedure documents that should be published by the SAP Security team to standardize changes to the SAP landscape. Those procedures are audited in this same manner. With an understanding of how the auditing is done and why, it is easy to see why such standards and procedures documents are beneficial to the business, as well as to the technical teams

9.2   Governance of cloud or hybrid cloud environments

Governance of cloud and hybrid cloud environments adds an additional layer of requirements. The policies, standards and procedures applied to in-house systems also apply, in part, to a cloud or hybrid cloud situation. Additional policies, standards, and procedures are required for a cloud situation, and the audit documentation from a cloud provider is of key importance in deciding which provider to use and in maintaining that relationship. Contracts with cloud providers include clauses relating to failed audits, and provide grounds to sever the relationship; any associated financial liability is also included. A cloud provider must be able to prove they are following all the best security processes in order to keep their customer base safe. A company engaging a cloud provider must review the audit information annually in order to prove they are managing the risk of outsourcing data and processes.

9.2.1   Audit documentation

There are several different types of audit documentation for cloud environments. The key document types are:

► SOC 1 (also Statement on Standards for Attestation Engagements no.16 (SSAE16))—a report on internal controls over financial reporting

► SOC 2—an audit report prepared by an external audit firm for an organization's information systems relating to security, availability, processing integrity, confidentiality or privacy, processes and controls tests, and test reporting

► SOC 3—an audit report similar to SOC 2 but excluding the testing, and commonly used for marketing purposes

An SOC 2 is the primary evaluation report needed by the team. The reports usually covers six or twelve months. Unless it is the first time the company is doing it. In that case, it may be a three-month study at the start, with the intention of doing a full six or twelve month report thereafter.

The criteria that are tested for the generation of this report are:

- ▶ Security policy
- ▶ Security awareness and communication
- ▶ Risk assessment
- ▶ Threat identification
- ▶ Information classification
- ▶ Logical access
- ▶ Physical access
- ▶ Security monitoring
- ▶ Incident management
- ▶ Encryption
- ▶ Personnel
- ▶ Systems development and maintenance
- ▶ Configuration management
- ▶ Change management
- ▶ Monitoring and compliance
- ▶ Disaster recovery
- ▶ Backup and restoration
- ▶ Environmental controls
- ▶ Confidentiality policy
- ▶ Confidentiality of inputs, data processing and outputs
- ▶ Information disclosure

When reviewing one of these reports, the standard items to look for are:

- ▶ Any exceptions in testing are clearly explained and corrected.
- ▶ The audit company states that they are certified.
- ▶ The network is redundant.

- ▶ Servers are highly available.

- ▶ A disaster recovery plan and process is in place.

- ▶ Back-ups are successful.

- ▶ Intrusion detection and response is sound.

9.2.2 Cloud security vendor evaluation criteria

When selecting a cloud vendor, providing the information outlined below to the evaluation team will speed up the evaluation process. If any items are unknown, then provide the name of a contact person in the security team who can be contacted to help answer the open questions.

Consider the following questions when evaluating providers:

- ▶ What are the project/application requirements?

- ▶ Will this application be connected to internal systems in real time, and if so, what systems?

- ▶ What is the sensitivity level of the data being stored or manipulated by this application?

- ▶ Are there HIPAA considerations?

- ▶ Is there EU/German data involved?

- ▶ What are the uptime requirements (i.e., what will be the business impact if the application is unavailable for more than an hour)?

Documentation is required for the evaluation. Audit reports that are needed by the Cloud Security Review team include one or more of the following: SOC 1, SOC 2, SOC 3, and SSAE 16.

The standard questions you need to ask when reviewing the audit reports are:

- ▶ Are any exceptions in testing clearly explained and corrected?

- ▶ Does the external audit company state that they are certified?

- ▶ Is the network redundant?

- ▶ Are the servers highly available?

- ▶ Is there a disaster recovery plan and process in place?

- ▶ Are the backups good?

▶ Are the intrusion detection and response systems and processes sound?

▶ Is the data storage safe harbor certified?

Issues to consider in Germany and the EU are as follows:

▶ Works councils and unions

▶ Data privacy laws, such as the GDPR

▶ Data storage locations—data storage must comply with the EU privacy directive in the GDPR

9.3 Leveraging SAP GRC Access Control to monitor security compliance

The SAP Access Control module is built to perform segregation of duties monitoring This process uses a customized rule set that looks for financial and critical transaction risks. It is intended to alert for issues regarding segregation of duties, and enables the business to create mitigating controls. A *mitigating control* is a written reason why someone has to do the two conflicting tasks, who is watching them, and how it is being monitored. One of the benefits of this module is that it differentiates between *potential risk*, where a user has access to create and pay a vendor, versus *actual risk*, where the usage history shows that a user has created and paid a vendor.

As part of this risk management it is important to ensure that the rule set at the heart of this risk analysis engine is up-to-date and accurate. This includes adding custom transactions to risks in the rule set where applicable, and keeping the critical transactions up-to-date with new systems, landscape types, and processes. *Critical transactions* are usually anything that has to do with the system itself, mass change, opening and closing periods, most risky basis and security transactions, and direct table maintenance.

Leveraging tools

Leveraging the tools at hand to do more than initially planned for is an opportunity to get the best value for the investment, automate work and save time. Out-of-the-box creative thinking opens the door to opportunities to streamline in ways you might not have expected.

So far, we have looked at the standard processes and functionality of the SAP GRC Access Control module. If we think about the access control risk analysis engine from the perspective that it is a tool that analyzes anything in a rule book and flags the risks, then this opens the use to include monitoring non-financial risk.

An audit rulebook can be created to answer questions raised by the auditors, such as:

► Who has direct table maintenance and who has used it?

► Who has opened the system?

► Who has access to display critical tables with confidential data?

► Who has maintained number ranges?

► Who has deleted table information from specific tables?

► Who has downloaded mass amounts of information from confidential transactions or tables?

If there is a rulebook containing these transactions and authorization object combinations that allow users to perform these tasks, then auditors or security analysts who are monitoring system vulnerabilities will be able to look up who has access and who actually carried out these high-risk activities.

10 SAP Security Notes

SAP Security Notes are the communication tool used by SAP to notify its customers of system and application vulnerabilities. Security Notes should be reviewed monthly and the Security Spotlight News page should be checked every Tuesday for new entries in the list of most urgent notes.

10.1 Security Notes review process

Security Notes are reviewed for all development systems via the following process:

▶ Review the Security Notes on SAP's website at: *support.sap.com/ securitynotes.*

▶ Review Security Spotlight News (previously Security Hot News) in the SAP Support Portal to learn about the latest urgent security issues for SAP.

▶ Review and export data from the Security Notes and compile the missing notes in an excel workbook.

▶ Compile a list of outstanding notes for each system. Be sure to check for dependencies or additional related notes listed in the note text or under the THIS DOCUMENT REFERS TO tab (see Figure 10.1).

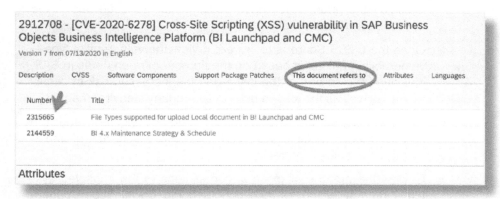

Figure 10.1: Security Note dependency

All notes listed in these areas should be downloaded and reviewed, especially those that discuss side effects and remediation. The security notes can be related to other SAP notes, not always security, that need to be reviewed and considered for implementation. Each pdf file for the notes needs to downloaded for review by the SAP Security Team. The number of open notes in SAP Marketplace also needs to be reviewed in order to determine the vulnerability proliferation ranking by number of open notes. In addition, the CVSS SCORE on the Security Notes (see Figure 10.2) is categorized by CVSS Score, type of issue, company-specific risk scoring and environment impact, and which systems they need to be installed on.

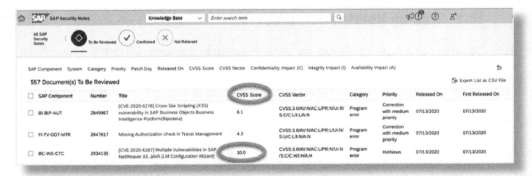

Figure 10.2: CVSS score on Security Notes

There are a number of important points to consider when reviewing the notes to determine the risk profile for your environment:

▶ First, review the CVSS score for the note—CVSS scoring by SAP indicates the priority they have assigned to the issue and is the baseline for decision making.

▶ Once the CVSS Score is reviewed, review the vulnerability type— vulnerability ranking is based on the number of open notes in SAP, indicating the spread of the issue and the increased risk of occurrence, as well as the known risks in a company's environment.

▶ Take into consideration the number of systems impacted—does the note go across multiple systems? If so, the importance of implementing the notes is increased.

▶ Review the number of external connections to the impacted system—internet facing, or accepting/sending downloads. Connections between servers have very little security. External connections are more secure, but if a hacker penetrates the external software, they can use the connection to get into the company system. Once in, they are able to execute anything on RFC, anywhere.

▶ Check for risky background users (RFC vulnerabilities)—roles for background IDs become a consideration when reviewing notes. If the role assigned to the background ID has broad security assigned and open RFC names and programs, the risk to the system is higher.

▶ Monitor the number of notes for the specific issue, regardless of priority or score—if there is more than one note for a specific issue or category of issue, the need to implement all notes should increase because the number of issues in that category increases the overall risk in the system.

▶ Be aware of the number of users—if it is a user facing problem, how many users are impacted?

▶ Understand the potential for business interruption or user impact at the transactional level—does it impact users, impact executable transactions or programs, or touch current workflow or background business processes?

Once the notes are reviewed with the above criteria, the Basis and Security teams need to review all notes to see if they have any concerns.

Notes that have specific module issues, such as Financial Accounting and Controlling (FICO), Sales and Distribution (SD), and Materials Management, should be reviewed by the functional team leader for those areas.

Once the decision has been made on which notes to apply and what the production implementation process should be, a help desk ticket should be opened to track the implementation, PDF note content, and approvals for testing and implementation.

The SAP Security Architect creates the appropriate transports for each set of notes.

The basis team needs to follow the instructions to install all the notes.

After installation, the transports are approved and moved to the quality assurance systems. Notes with urgent priority that are for missing authorization checks, specific transactions/authorization objects or information disclosure, and those where specific test scenarios can be developed, should be tested and moved to production as quickly as possible.

Urgent notes for all other issues should be implemented and moved into production as quickly as possible.

Non-urgent notes remain in the quality assurance system for one month to six weeks. This aging process acts as a test because other project teams are running projects and acceptance testing in those systems, and any issues will arise during that period.

After the approved time period, the transports are promoted to production.

10.2 Vulnerability scoring decision matrix

When building a vulnerability scoring decision matrix, there are some key items to take into consideration. First, how many notes exist in SAP currently for a particular risk? The number of notes indicates the proliferation of the risk throughout the code base and is used to raise or lower the priority of how soon to implement it in the system. Once the risks are ordered by number of notes and ranking, specific issues in your system need to be considered, such as:

- ▶ Are you using secure, trusted RFCs?
- ▶ Is the role your RFC ID uses secured down to the authorized program names that have access as well as specific table names?
- ▶ How many connections are there to external sites, cloud applications, and virtual desktop environments?
- ▶ Are there security considerations—either tight security around key objects or unlimited access to key objects?

These considerations influence the decision to increase the priority of the implementation of notes relating to those specific risks.

10.2.1 Scoring analysis process

This section provides an example of a vulnerability scoring analysis. The risks, which were previously defined in Chapter 6, and their analyses are outlined in Table 10.1, listed in order from most frequently to least frequently found in SAP Security Notes.

Risk	Rank	Considerations	Recommendation
Cross-site scripting (XSS)	1	Low user impact. Many connections to cloud and internet applications. Unsecured RFC IDs	Increase priority
Code injection	2	Low user impact Many connections to cloud and internet applications Unsecured RFC IDs	Increase priority
Missing authorization checks	3	Higher potential for impact. Requires teams other than SAP Security and basis to review and test.	No change
Privilege escalation	4	Lower potential—common at application installation.	No change
Information disclosure	5	User impact is determined by customer policy on S_DEVELOP in production. If this is rare, or is not allowed, user impact will be low.	No change
SQL injection	6	Low user impact. Many connections to cloud and internet applications. Unsecured RFC IDs.	Increase priority
Directory traversal	7	Many connections to cloud and internet applications. Unsecured RFC IDs.	Increase priority

Risk	Rank	Considerations	Recommen- dation
Hard- coded creden- tials	8	Low user impact. Users with the access already will not see an impact, only those using the application with- out it being directly assigned to them. Many connections to cloud and internet applications. Unsecured RFC IDs.	No change
Click- jacking	9	Low user impact. Many connections to cloud and internet applications. Unsecured RFC IDs.	No change
Authen- tication bypass	10	Low user impact. Many connections to cloud and internet applications. Unsecured RFC IDs	Increase priority
Unres- tricted file upload	11	Low user impact.	No change
Verb tampering	12	Low user impact. Many connections to cloud and internet applications. Unsecured RFC IDs.	No change
Content spoofing, phishing	13	Low user impact.	No Change

Table 10.1: Risks and vulnerability scoring analysis

Most of the risks listed above were outlined in Chapter 6. However some additional risks have been listed here, and are defined as follows:

► *Privilege escalation* is a vulnerability that allows in the code allowing hackers to increase their own security, or inherit privileges from other applications, hardcoded authorizations, or other vulnerabilities.

► *Clickjacking*, also known as UI (User Interface) redress attack, or UI redressing, is a malicious technique whereby users are tricked into clicking on something they believe is harmless, such as a web page. Potentially confidential information is then revealed and the attacker can then take control of the user's computer. This vulnerability is a browser security issue that is across a variety of browsers and platforms.

► An *unrestricted file upload* allows an attacker to upload any file (including script files) without proper file format validation.

► *Content spoofing* and/or *phishing* is when a website is presented to a user as legitimate but is controlled by hackers to defraud individuals or companies.

When reviewing the notes according to the vulnerability scoring process, you can create a scorecard of the CVSS scores that SAP has assigned to the notes (see Figure 10.3). A good way to assess the risks is to develop risk reporting designed to look at the number notes associated with critical, high, medium, and low risks in the system.

Scorecard				
SAP	CVSSv3	Change	Classification	CVSS Score
Critical	0		Critical	9.0 - 10
High	8		High	7.0-9
Medium	27		Medium	4.0 - 6.9
Low	2		Low	0 - 3.9

Figure 10.3: Risk scorecard

This scorecard shows the number of notes in each category. The Change column indicates recommendations to increase priority. If there are multiple cross-site scripting notes, and the recommendation due to system conditions is to increase the priority of all notes associated with that risk, then those notes are moved up a category via the Change column.

This decision-making matrix is the reporting tool for moving the risks found in the SAP Landscape into any standard risk heat map or reporting method used by the security operations team. Once the notes are prioritized, it is then up to the different functional and technical teams to review the notes associated with their modules to determine if there are any implementation risks, and what testing processes should be used.

Why a scorecard or heatmap

 Scorecards and heatmaps are a tool to translate the highly technical language of risk into a format that the decision makers in the business can act upon quickly. It is a method used to measure progress in risk remediation programs or new risk introduced by upgrades, new function modules or third party software installations.

11 Communication security

SAP communicates externally via a number of different methods. The majority of the communication configuration is done by the basis team. In this chapter, we will focus on the SAP Security team's responsibilities regarding communications into, and out of, an SAP landscape.

11.1 Remote Function Call (RFC)

SAP uses RFC and ICF (Internet Communication Framework) to communicate. It is important to understand the RFC and ICF security fundamentals in order to safely manage the 1104 transactions and programs that use RFC in ECC. The communication can be to another server inside the datacenter, to a connected device on the network, or out to a cloud-based resource. When communicating to a non-SAP application or data source, configuration is required to use APIs to translate back and forth between the communication partners.

Never use an asterisk

The most important point here is to never put a * in any field in an RFC or ICF authorization object.

RFC and ICF authorizations should be thoroughly defined to protect the communications channels from corruption and to protect against zero-day vulnerabilities and attacks.

There are different types of RFC, including trusted RFC and queued RFC (qRFC). In terms of security, these all use the same set of authorization objects. We will now review the different objects, their fields, what options can be used in those fields, and how that connects to the RFC setup at a high level.

S_RFC is the primary authorization object for remote function calls (see Figure 11.1). It uses ACTIVITY 16 (execute) along with a whitelist of objects and the type of object.

Figure 11.1: RFC authorization

RFC_NAME is the name of the object that can communicate through the object. Putting a * in this field is only recommended for initial configuration and testing. A security guide should be available for any new module or add-on, and has the RFC names listed in it. In cases where it does not, putting a * in the RFC_NAME field and turning on tracing enables all objects that need to be populated in this named whitelist field to be identified. From a cybersecurity perspective, leaving a * in this field is not recommended because it opens a channel where hackers can send anything into the SAP system.

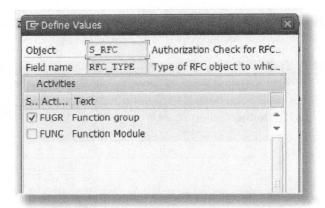

Figure 11.2: RFC type

RFC_TYPE defines what kind of object is executable on the whitelist—a FUNCTION GROUP or a FUNCTION MODULE (see Figure 11.2).

S_RFC_ADM is the administrative authorization object for RFCs (see Figure 11.3). It defines what the RFC can do, what connection it uses and what RFC type it is. The screenshot shows an example of what not to do, because the * access creates unlimited authority in the role.

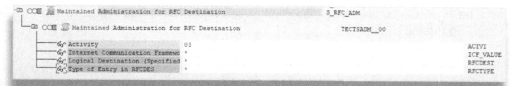

Figure 11.3: RFC administration authorization

11.2 Internet Connection Framework (ICF)

The Internet Connection Framework (ICF) and logical destination are set up by the basis team and should be individually declared in the ICF_VALUE and RFCDEST fields. Even in a display situation, having a * in these fields is risky.

With RFCTYPE, there is a dropdown list to select what kinds of connections will be handled by this authorization object entry (see Figure 11.4).

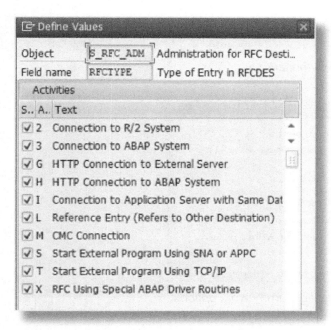

Figure 11.4: RFC type selection options

The S_RFCACL object defines client, user, and system information when using trusted clients (see Figure 11.5).

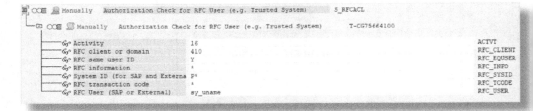

Figure 11.5: RFC ACL authorization

The S_ICF Internet Communication Framework authorization defines how the communication is managed for the user through the connection (see Figure 11.6) ICF_FIELD is populated via a dropdown list and the OBJECT field is entered manually (see Figure 11.7).

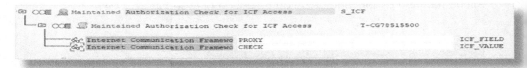

Figure 11.6: RFC ICF authorization

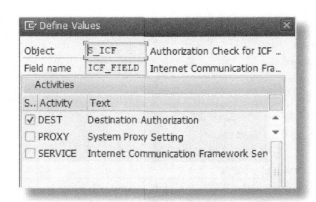

Figure 11.7:Communications framework options

The S_ICF_ADM authorization manages communication administration (see Figure 11.8). It defines what is being done, and defines the host and alias information. The ICF_TYPE (see Figure 11.9) defines what type of connection is being used—internal, external or virtual.

Figure 11.8: ICF administration authorization

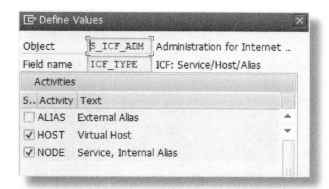

Figure 11.9: IFC service options

More information about trusted connections between systems can be found in the SAP Service Marketplace by searching for "RFC Communication" or "Trust Relationships between SAP Systems". Clear and thorough completion of all fields in these objects is critical for securing communications channels and protecting the data from external threats.

12 Critical authorization objects

A key part of managing critical information in SAP is to understand what authorization objects are crucial, what transactions they are associated with, and what is at risk through those authorization objects. This chapter will break down these authorization objects and how to understand what the risk is.

Authorization objects are reused across transactions in SAP. Understanding the ones that are the most critical to system security helps in the overall management of it. It is important to understand that not only system administration transactions use these critical objects. The risk arises when a transaction used by the business brings in one of these objects and the object is not treated with the same security concern as a system administration transaction.

The key point to note is that all transactions, authorizations, fields and values are read into the *user buffer* together. The user buffer is the section of memory that contains all the information about the user and the permissions they have in an SAP system. The buffer does not differentiate which transaction brought in which field and value. When authorizations and fields are brought in, the field with the most open authorization value is the one that is used for everything. In other words, in all things, the * wins. This means that authorizations that are carefully populated to reduce risk are wiped out by any instance of that same authorization coming in with a *.

It is not an SAP Security analyst's job to understand every transaction, authorization and field value. What is important is that analysts understand what happens when things come together in the user buffer and are able to offer guidance for developers and configuration analysts. The most important thing that SAP Security analysts need to understand is what the high-risk authorizations are and why they are a risk. It is not necessary to understand the most finite details; a high-level understanding makes a big difference in developing secure roles and protecting SAP from both internal and external threats.

Table 12.1 provides a list of these high-risk authorization objects, indicating the authorization objects, their descriptions and why they are critical. The risks addressed in this list cover issues involving confidentiality of data, integrity of data, database, operating system, viruses, and malware or other external programs that can be deposited in the system outside of change-control processes.

Authorization object	Description	Risk
B_LSM	LSMW—transaction and activity	Mass change tool
B_LSMW_PRO	LSMW—Project	Mass change tool
B_MASSMAIN	Cross-application mass maintenance	Mass change tool
B_USERSTAT	Status management— set/delete user status	User administration— personal information and audit history
F_BKPF_BUK	Accounting document— authorization for company codes	Financial master data
F_BKPF_KOA	Accounting document— authorization for account types	Financial master data
F_KNA1_BUK	Customer—authorization for company	Financial master data
F_LFA1_BUK	Vendor— authorization for company	Financial master data
P_ORGIN – HR	Master	Human Resources master data access
P_PERNR – HR	Master data—personnel number check	Human Resources master data access
S_ADMI_FCD	System	System administration
S_ARCHIVE	Archiving	Archive administration
S_BCSETS – BC	Set authorization object	Configuration of modules
S_BDC_MONI	Batch input authorizations	Batch maintenance— confidential jobs administration
S_BDS_D – BC-SRV-KPR-BDS	Authorizations for accessing documents	Document confidentiality
S_BDS_DS – BC-SRV-KPR-BDS	Authorizations for document set	Document confidentiality

Authorization object	Description	Risk
S_BTCH_ADM	Background processing— background administrator	Batch maintenance— confidential jobs administration
S_BTCH_JOB	Background processing— operations on background jobs	Batch maintenance— confidential jobs administration
S_BTCH_NAM	Background processing— background user name	Batch maintenance— confidential jobs administration
S_C_FUNCT	C calls in ABAP programs	Calls to non-SAP programs
S_CLNT_IMP	Data import for client copy	Client copy—mass data import
S_CTS_ADMI	Administration functions in change and transport system	Change control
S_DATASET	Authorization for file access	Access to files outside of SAP
S_DEVELOP	ABAP Workbench	Program create, change
S_DOKU_AUT	SE61 Documentation maintenance authorization	Document confidentiality, changes could expose confidential information
S_IMG_ACTV – IMG	Authorization to perform functions in IMG	Change control
S_LDAP	Authorization to access LDAP directory	Can expose personal information
S_LOG_COM	Authorization to execute logical operating system commands	Executing commands outside of SAP
S_NUMBER	Number range maintenance	Changing number ranges, deleting number ranges, fraud
S_PROGRAM – ABAP	Program flow checks	Executing programs— possiblity of virus, data loss or fraud

103

Authorization object	Description	Risk
S_QUERY	SAP query authorization	Data confidentiality
S_RFC	Authorization check for RFC access	Hacker can penetrate through RFC
S_RFC_ADM	Administration for RFC destination	Hacker can penetrate through RFC
S_RFCACL	Authorization check for RFC user (e.g., trusted system)	Hacker can penetrate through RFC
S_SPO_ACT	Spool—actions	Unauthorized viewing or reprinting of spools, such as check runs or confidential data
S_SPO_DEV	Spool—device authorizations	Unauthorized viewing or reprinting of spools—redirecting print jobs, breaching confidentiality
S_TABU_CLI	Cross-client table maintenance	Database corruption
S_TABU_DIS	Table maintenance (using standard tools such as SM30)	Data corruption, confidentiality
S_TABU_NAM	Table access by generic standard tools	Data corruption, confidentiality
S_TABU_RFC	Client comparison and copy—data export with RFC	Breach of data confidentiality due to data export out of the system
S_TRANSPRT	Transport organizer	Change control
S_USER_ADM	Administration functions for user/authorization administration	User administration—personal information and audit history
S_USER_AGR	Authorizations—role check	User administration—personal information and audit history
S_USER_AUT	User master maintenance—authorizations	User administration—personal information and audit history

Authorization object	Description	Risk
S_USER_GRP	User master mainte-nance—user groups	User administration—personal information and audit history
S_USER_OBJ	Globally deactivate authorization objects in a client	User administration—personal information and audit history
S_USER_PRO	User master mainte-nance—authorization profile	User administration—personal information and audit history
S_USER_SYS	Master maintenance—system for central user maintenance	User administration—personal information and audit history
S_USER_TCD	Authorizations—trans-actions in roles	User administration—personal information and audit history
S_USER_VAL	Authorizations—field values in roles	User administration—personal information and audit history
V_KNA1_VKO	Customer—authoriza-tion for sales organiza-tions	Customer master corruption, private customer information can be exposed
V_VBAK_VKO	Sales document—au-thorization for sales areas	Data confidentiality

Table 12.1: Authorization objects and associated risks

This list of risks provides an overview of what to look for and why incorrect configuration creates risks. It also helps to see the authorizations, trans-actions and roles that can be impacted if an SAP Security Note references specific code, authorizations or functional areas. For example, having full access to authorization objects managing file access at the operating system level creates a high risk when coupled with a cross-site scripting vulnerability.

13 Information security for data at rest

Managing user access in production environments is the foundation of SAP security. The next layer of risk involves data at rest outside of the production environments.

Production SAP systems are secured, managed and monitored closely for confidentiality, fraud risk, and data integrity. Unmanaged risk arises when system copies are made for data refresh in quality assurance or test systems. These systems can contain all the same data as the production systems, but are not monitored.

13.1 Types of data

As mentioned previously, data at rest is becoming a new focus area for cybersecurity. There are best practices to tighten security on master data, vendor masters, customer masters, and employee data. Understanding the risks to master data and other critical data types during a copyback, and in any non-production scenarios, is extremely important for any cybersecurity program.

What is master data?

Master data is one of the most important assets of any company, and refers to specific data types, that when combined, form the core of business profitability and risk. Managing the quality of the individual master data elements is a key business initiative, and securing the master data requires a skilled team.

Master data includes vendor information such as vendor contact data, purchase order history, pricing, contracts, and bank account information which is retained for accepting electronic payments and issuing refunds.

It also includes customer information such as customer contact data, sales order history, prices, contracts, and bank account information.

Employee information is also part of master data and includes: employee contact data, HIPAA data, benefits information, dependent information, bank account information retained for direct deposit payroll and expense reimbursement, and credit cards issued to employees for company purchases and travel expenses.

Master data also consists of corporate product information such as financials, ledgers, bank information, stock information, profit and loss information, new product development, existing product specifications, formulations, BOMs, recipes, project data, material lists, and process documents.

Master data are corporate crown jewels of data

 Master data is considered to be the crown jewels of corporate data. It is the key information for every process and product for a company. Corruption or theft of master data are very high risks to a company.

13.2 Threats and risks

Threat actors are people or automated programs that gain malicious, unauthorized access into a system, including: hackers, nation-state actors, corporate spies, fraudulent or disgruntled employees, outsourced resources and contractors.

What are the risks to company data?

The risks include:

► Compromised vendor bank accounts and customer bank accounts

► Compromised employee identities (and their family members' identities), and compromised employee bank accounts

► Stolen corporate financials, stock information, intellectual property, processes, and trade secrets

13.2.1 Data categories

All data within a system falls into three high-level data categories (see Figure 13.1): data in use, data in motion, and data at rest. Data at rest is often disconnected from the usual processes and protection is only granted to data in use and data in motion.

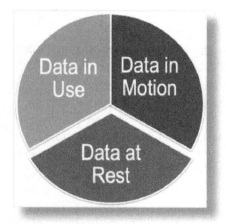

Figure 13.1: Data types

Data in use is active data, currently being used for business functionality. Some examples of this include: current month financials, payroll, sales orders, and purchase orders. Protection methods for data in use include user authentication, user access security, mitigating control reports, and approval processes.

Data in motion refers to data being transported at any moment in time. Examples of this include: active transactions, bank transfers, and external data transfers (e.g. Cloud, RFC, internal devices). The protection methods for data in motion include: encryption, secure transfer protocols, user authentication and user access security.

Data at rest refers to inactive data, which has been generated or used in business processes, but which is currently not in use, is rarely used, or is currently closed. Some examples of this are: archives, closed sales orders, closed purchase orders, closed previous financial months/years, online backups, copybacks for quality assurance and development environments, and disaster recovery sites. One protection method for data at rest is *obscurity* (lack of knowledge of its existence).

Data in use and data in motion receive the most scrutiny throughout the data lifecycle and there are clear authentication methods and risk management processes. Data at rest is not scrutinized and managed in most situations because the data is considered old and therefore not important to

109

current business requirements. The problem with this is that while the data may be older, it does not mean it is not still accurate data. The age of the data does not diminish the risk if the information is still current regarding the financial state, vendors, customers, employees, or products

Risks to data at rest

 The risks to data at rest are the same as other data, but because it is not being used regularly, any issues with the data are not noticed in a timely manner. When looking in detail at system copies used for testing purposes, the risks are compounded when new roles or expanded testing access is given to users in those systems.

Data obfuscation is a process where data in the database is deliberately scrambled. There is significant risk where this does not exist, potentially exposing confidential personal or business information. Data at risk, that should be hidden, includes bank accounts, vendor and customer data, and employee PII data, which are available to be accessed offline.

Another risk arises where there is no monitoring of data access, use, downloading or exfiltration.

In addition, if production users' IDs are available in non-production environments, there is a further risk to data. This includes IDs for contractors and outsourced resources. This data is valuable and could be downloaded and sold, or used for other purposes.

Further risks are possible where there is expanded access in quality assurance and development systems. Expanded access may be granted in test or quality assurance systems, with the intention being to enable new functionality to be tested. The risk is that users are then also able to access information not previously in their scope of work, thereby creating risk to that data.

The tools and techniques available for resolving the problem of governing and protecting will be outlined in the next section.

13.3 Tools and techniques for protecting data at rest

There are several techniques available to assist in managing and protecting data at rest. They fall into three categories:

1. Awareness and policy

2. Data categorization

3. Available tools

The first step in managing data at rest in these categories is to ask key questions and propose solutions that fall into the cybersecurity program model.

13.3.1 Awareness and policy

A risk analysis is required for data at risk, including an evaluation of the systems, locations, and access points. The key questions to address are:

▶ What are the systems containing data at rest?—online archives, copied systems, disaster recovery sites, online backups, offline backups?

▶ What external access is there to these systems?—cloud application test systems, external data transfer points, RFC?

▶ What are these systems used for?—e. g., in testing, who has access, are these systems common knowledge?

A clear policy needs to be created to manage data at rest. The key questions to ask are:

▶ Is there an access management process in place for these systems?

▶ Who maintains key password data, and is this monitored?

▶ Is there a data retention policy for the lifespan and retirement of old data/systems?

The policies used to manage this data can include:

▶ Removing all user IDs, and only retaining administration and developer IDs

▶ Removing all roles from user IDs and re-granting access on an as-needed basis, with the same approval process used for production systems

▶ Removing the non-production systems from the SAP GUI and other login processes

▶ Required use of system logging and review of the logs.

13.3.2 Data categorization

To categorize the data, companies need to identify the critical master data/ data elements to be secured, and ascertain who makes these decisions and what the value of the data is to the business. You need to work with the business to determine what the critical data elements are that need to be secured; this includes speaking with your finance, sales, product design and build, and human resources teams.

In addition, there needs to be an awareness of the problem, and an engagement process is required for all new projects. You should consider a data categorization project to prioritize the level of security in your organization.

To determine who should have access to the different categorizations of data, ask the following questions:

▶ Who should have access to the different categorizations of data?

▶ What is the purpose of securing this data, and who should maintain what levels of access?

▶ What data should be entirely obfuscated in offline scenarios?

13.3.3 Available tools

The data security and monitoring tools that are implemented should be the same tools used for the production environment. The following questions need to be addressed:

▶ What are we using to secure the production data?

▶ How are we monitoring production environments?

▶ What tools do we already have that could be leveraged and what tools are available to augment what is already in place?

▶ What tools are required to secure and monitor data at rest?

There are several tools available for securing and monitoring data at rest: SAP GRC Access Control, SAP GRC Process Control, User Interface Logging, Field Masking and Solution Manager

SAP GRC Access Control

SAP GRC (Governance, Risk, and Compliance) Access Control is an SAP module that enables user-access provisioning. It can be used for production and non-production environments. Implementing approved provisioning of expanded access in non- production environments reduces the risk to data at rest. It enables transaction usage and access to non-production systems to be monitored.

Implementing the Emergency Access Management (Firefighter) portion of GRC Access Control manages the most critical data access in non-production systems. This can be used to protect high-risk data.

Creating a rule set in the GRC Risk Analysis engine to monitor critical transactions in non-production systems uses the risk engine to populate reports in GRC, which monitors the access and use of high-risk transactions in non-production systems

SAP GRC Process Control

GRC Process Control is an SAP module for process automation and is a sign-off tool that can be used to manage risk. It is a process engine so it can be used to store disaster-recovery records and disaster-recovery test sign-offs, manage Solution Manager patch control and project management tasks, and manage the review and remediation of Early Watch reports. The benefit is a centralized location for all documentation, task management and sign-off for these critical processes.

SAP User Interface Logging

User Interface Logging (UIL) is an SAP tool that logs all data entered by, and displayed to, users. It also provides log analysis tools and alerts for suspicious activities. The application writes to a temporary log that is stored for later analysis. The UIL can be used for monitoring high-risk data processes, outsourced resources, and high-risk positions and users. The tool is configured by specifically including at-risk users, roles, profiles and groups, and can be used in production and non-production environments.

For more information, refer to the SAP Help Portal and search for "UI Logging".

Field Masking

Field Masking is an SAP tool which provides data obfuscation at the field level. It masks specific fields from a user's view. It can mask, clear, hide, and disable fields for users who do not have specific authorization to view the data. The tool is configured to manage field level access to a user's authorization and traces when a user accesses a field configured for masking. This tool can be used in production and non-production systems.

For more information, refer to the SAP Help Portal and search for "Field Masking".

Solution Manager

SAP Solution Manager is used to perform administrative management for all other landscapes. Early Watch Reports inform users about critical situations and provide solutions to improve security, stability and performance. These reports come from Solution Manager and are part of the SOLMAN detection process for system and user issues. They can be set up to run against both production and non-production systems. The results of these reports should be reviewed and remediated monthly.

13.4 Cybersecurity program integration

Securing data at rest is an important component of an overall cybersecurity program. The processes of creating a system to manage data at rest utilizes all the elements of a cybersecurity program. These elements were explained earlier in Chapter 2 and are shown again here in Figure 13.2.

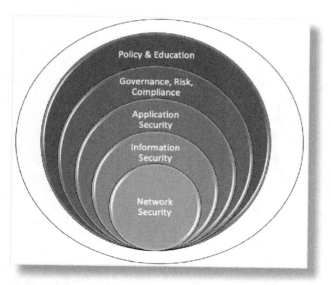

Figure 13.2: Elements of a cybersecurity program

It helps to holistically look at the cybersecurity program architecture and see how it relates to the management of data at rest. We will now cover how data at rest should be managed within the program, at each layer:

▶ **Policy and education**—there needs to be a data classification policy, a data retention and retirement policy, and a disaster recovery policy; and employees need to be educated about these.

▶ **Governance, risk and compliance**—you need to carefully manage offline data user access, control the offline data retention periods, and manage expanded access in non-production environments.

▶ **Application security**—approvals should be required for user provisioning for non-production environments, all unapproved user IDs should be locked after copybacks from production, and you need to review which users have expanded access in QA and Dev environments.

▶ **Information security**—there needs to be data obfuscation of critical data in non-production environments, archiving and purging of old/unused data, and encryption of offline data and datastores (HANA).

▶ **Network security**—be sure to know all the connections that exist between non-production systems and the rest of the world; remove connectivity from non-production copied systems to external environments (deactivate connectors, external facing communications user IDs), and close RFC connections.

115

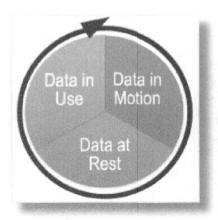

Figure 13.3: Integrated protection

Using a methodical approach to security data, as shown in Figure 13.3, brings data at rest into a holistic data security model. The first step is awareness. Once awareness has been fully achieved, the tools and policies already in place for production systems can be expanded to manage non-production systems.

Data classification is key to knowing what data should be obfuscated. Users with access to production systems do not automatically need access to non-production systems. Good practices include locking out those IDs, or not copying the user master record during a system copy from production systems to non-production systems..

Data at rest is as much a risk in non-production systems as in production systems, and is as important to secure. Business participation in identification and classification of master data is key to securing data at rest. Using existing production data security policies, programs, and tools to manage data at rest is the first step in reducing risk. Data masking and monitoring of use in non-production systems prevents offline data from being breached.

Just because users have access to the production data does not mean they should have access to copied systems. Users should have to request access to a non-production system in the same as they would for a production system. The administrative team can use the same access control processes as in production systems. The mitigating controls and monitoring processes used for production systems are not present in non-production systems, therefore the risk is greater.

14 Preparing for new technology

The current rate of technological improvements and adoption of these requires SAP to be prepared, at any time, to manage the implementation of new modules, bolt-ons, and connectivity.

New technology adoption brings its own set of risks into any system, but can be integrated using the same new program development process used by ABAP developers.

Include the security team

 The SAP Security team needs to be brought into the project at the initial stages when requirements are being gathered and discussed. The security team can bring connectivity, security, compliance, and user access knowledge into these requirements discussions.

Once requirements are gathered and a solution is chosen, the security team should be provided with a security guide to the new technology being implemented. Security guides should be provided with any bolt-on code or new hardware device being implemented in the environment. These guides provide the security team with information on connectivity, transactions, authorizations, RFC programs, and any custom code that needs to be integrated into the environment.

When reviewing the security guide the security team should address the following key questions:

▶ What development class or area does the new code reside in?

▶ What master data areas does it create, change or display?

▶ What standard or custom authorization objects are used and what are the risks?

▶ Should the new transactions or authorizations be integrated into existing roles or placed into new, stand-alone roles for the new technology?

▶ Are there high-risk authorization objects or transactions included?

- Are any transactions currently in use being replaced by this new technology and what do those role changes look like?
- What users should have access, what is their current security assignment, and would new risks be opened up by adding the new transactions and authorizations?
- If new risks are opened up, what would be some potential ways to mitigate those risks?
- What would testing scenarios for security look like and when should that testing occur in the project timeline?
- What types of document artifacts will be needed by the auditors for security validation?
- What will the provisioning scenario be in production?
- How will troubleshooting be done when production issues occur with this new technology?

The answers to these questions become more complicated in distributed architecture situations, or in landscapes with overprovisioning of users or a large number of roles. In sizeable SAP implementations, with many landscapes, cross-system risks need to be considered.

The larger the new technology being adopted, the more complicated the security analysis and implementation becomes. In the case where landscapes are moving to SAP S/4HANA, it is worth performing an analysis of a complete security rebuild as part of the implementation. The high volume of transactions and business processes being replaced makes the process of removing all of them from existing roles a high risk to the project. The interdependency of authorization objects on one another means that when transactions and authorizations are removed from roles, especially large roles, other transactions may not perform in the same way. The risk of business interruption in a major set of role changes is the same as a full security rebuild in these situations, especially if there is no extensive 'day-in-the-life-of' testing performed.

The basic list of questions in this chapter should help to guide you with the implementation of new technology; and hopefully also trigger additional questions specific to the customizations that exist in every SAP implementation.

15 Audit preparation

In previous chapters, we talked at length about auditing. There are actions you can proactively take to ensure audit readiness and a successful audit. This chapter will cover some of these measures.

15.1 Framework

The first thing to understand is what framework your auditors are working in. Is there one for a financial audit only, or are there financial and security audits using separate frameworks? Financial audits can be done using the Sarbanes Oxley Act requirements, a COBIT framework, or a custom audit designed by an external audit company. Reach out to the internal audit or financial controller groups to obtain a copy of the last audit and any changes they are considering for the next one. Being prepared for what to look for and what they are going to ask as follow-up questions is key to having a successful audit.

15.2 Artifacts

Thorough audit artifacts should be obtained and retained so that they can easily be followed when working on projects, processes and implementations. Specifications relating to change requests should be detailed enough to be understood by non-technical users and should include information about who requested the change, who approved it, and when it is needed.

Create a project plan for any changes that are being made and that will be promoted to a production system. The plan could be as simple as a detailed bullet list on which start, finish and implementation dates can be stored, or as complex as a full scale project plan in project management software. Clearly define the requirements, what is being changed, when that change occurred and by whom, and all approvals up to implementation.

Create test scripts that include what is being tested, the data required, the testers, the test users, the testing due date, the requirements for testing screen shots (if they are required by the audit), and official sign-off within the document that the test was successful.

When making any changes to systems and processes that are used in the annual audit reviews, make sure those changes are documented, including screenshots that show the dates and time stamps of the changes. For any sign-off requirements, make sure this is done as a formal process, and in writing, with date and time stamp. This could involve saving email screenshots in the project documentation or saving emails in a project folder on a drive or collaboration site to ensure they are not purged from an email box due to time or space considerations.

15.3 Monthly checks

Several checks can be carried out, requiring only one or two hours a month, to catch problems before the auditors find them. Items such as change histories for users and independent profile assignments are good candidates for a monthly check. It is always better for the security team to find and remediate issues, or discover process-related issues and correct those through user training or system updates, than to discover the problems later.

15.4 Automated process checks

Perform spot-checks of process automations throughout the year. Make sure the processes that are automated in any way are working as intended, and that users have not found ways to bypass requirements; and ensure that all requirements for user input or documentation are being thoroughly completed. Auditors look for situations where users enter as little information into required fields as possible and, in the process, create an audit finding because there is not enough information to justify the request.

In these situations, the options are to contact the users that are not entering enough information and educate them on what is needed and why, or reach out to management for enforcement. It also reveals a requirement to program additional data validation for required fields to enforce the input of thorough information. This could involve adding fields that require specific information, or enforcing a minimum number of characters in existing required fields. Working through these kinds of process checks and process improvements, and thorough documentation of these tasks, can also be used as a remediation to an audit finding if issues are identified before process improvements have been implemented.

If there is an emergency or elevated access approval and review process, check to ensure that the required approvals are in place and the reviews are signed off and retained appropriately. Make sure there is thorough detail in the request for access, and spot check the audit log to see what was done and that it matches the request. Check to see that people responsible for reviewing and signing off are doing so in a timely manner and with sufficient detail in the sign-off.

15.5 User access reviews

Check roles that are assigned to users, especially users who are not logging in regularly. Review users in the system against a list of high-risk transactions, and for those users who have performed them, look at their last login date. If a user has highly sensitive access but only logs in occasionally, or is a backup to someone else, it would be a good idea to see if that access is still needed.

Expire users who have not logged in within 30, 60, or 90 days, depending on the sensitivity of the system. These users may have changed jobs in the company or the processes they are working with in their current job may have changed. Expiring them prevents their ID from being hacked or shared. It can be reactivated at a later date if needed. If, at the end of the year, a user has not used the ID, delete their ID and contact them to let them know it was deleted. If they require access again in the future, they will need to create a new access request.

15.6 User change history

Check the change history for all users in the system. Look for user access changes that have not been done by appropriate personnel, or for background user IDs. Look for any instances of addition and removal of SAP_ALL, SAP_NEW or any other profile without a role. These should immediately be removed, and if there is any history of them being added and then removed, an investigation should be launched into why this was done. This has to be thoroughly documented for the auditors. Checking this monthly and making sure that all users who can change a user ID know the process are valid mitigating controls for the future, and show the auditors that there is a proactive process to deter and catch any such occurrences.

15.7 Non-administrative user lockouts

Look for users who are locked out due to failed password attempts. See if there is any pattern in department or access. Look to see if there are any occurrences of users trying to log in under an ID that is not theirs This could be a situation of access-sharing, or an insider attempting to gain unauthorized information or commit fraud.

16 Risk management

In a global cybersecurity program, there are specific risk analysis and mitigation steps that can be taken to minimize breaches and financial loss. In this chapter, we will look at risk management and the steps to mitigate risk.

The goal of risk management is to reduce residual risk to an acceptable level. Determining the overall cost of a breach is a formulaic process that includes understanding the risk, the source and target of the risk, the financial value of the target asset, and how often a breach of that target happens. The process of performing a risk assessment includes preparing for the assessment and conducting a risk analysis. This process translates cyber risk into financial risk that can be understood and budgeted by the business. This is a very detailed process at the overall cybersecurity level. The maintenance of the SAP landscape feeds into that process, as we have seen throughout this book in discussing frameworks, processes and policy.

Risk reduction

There will always be a level of risk that a company needs to accept, but good risk mitigation strategies can greatly reduce that risk.

16.1 Mitigations

Risk mitigations are plans used to reduce the risk of a vulnerability and manage its impact. The desired end result of a mitigation is to reduce the level of acceptable risk to a point where the likelihood of an incident is as low as possible. The strategies to managing risk mitigation are:

▶ *Avoid*—avoiding the risk means choosing not to implement a risky business process or module.

▶ *Transfer*—transferring risk means outsourcing duties or using a cloud software or platform as a service. Risks associated with processes that are being transferred are also transferred to the new provider.

▶ *Reduce*—reducing risk includes the application of security notes, moving all users to a least privilege access model, locking out user IDs that are not being used, tightly controlling RFC access, as well as the other options we have discussed in this book.

▶ *Accept*—once all other options have been implemented, there will still be a level of residual risk that has to be accepted as part of doing business. This includes situations where there is a need for elevated access in systems, external connectivity, mobile device access, and circumstances where segregation of duties cannot be done.

Mitigating controls come into play, as much as possible, once the risk is reduced. A *mitigating control* is a detective process used to audit the systems to discover and prevent issues and errors. Some examples of mitigating controls we have already discussed include reviewing change histories for application and removal of SAP_ALL profiles, user access reviews, etc. The detailed audit reports already discussed can be automated by creating programs and background jobs to automatically run the audit reports and email them to the designated reviewers. This automation and review is an automated mitigating control to manage residual risk.

17 Conclusion

In the world of the Internet of Things, unlimited and uninterrupted availability of information is key to business performance. As SAP continues to evolve from its origins as a software package running in a datacenter to a globally integrated end-to-end business automation tool, the security of these systems is becoming a critical component of business risk management.

The intention of this book is to demystify cybersecurity, giving readers an understanding of what a cybersecurity program does, what security frameworks are used for, how to assess and understand risk, and how to apply mitigating controls.

A holistic view of cybersecurity, frameworks, and how they specifically apply to SAP, is important to understand how to secure SAP, whether it resides in a company-managed datacenter or in a cloud or hybrid cloud environment. The expansion of products and services available to, and via, SAP raises the importance of cybersecurity for business success and continuity.

It is my sincere hope that this book increases readers' understanding of cybersecurity and facilitates quality conversation between the business, auditors, and security and cybersecurity teams.

18 Appendix A: SAP Audit Logs

Audit class	Event class	Message ID	System log message text (before setting variables)	Cyber risk
Dialog logon	Critical	AU2	Logon failed (reason=&B, type=&A, method=&C)	Brute force password attack
Dialog logon	Critical	AUM	User &B locked in client &A after errors in password checks	Brute force password attack
Dialog logon	Critical	AUN	User &B unlocked in client &A after entering wrong password	Hacker accessed system and unlocked an account for their use—critical if the account had any administrative access
Dialog logon	Critical	BUD	WS: Delayed logon failed (type &B, WP &C). Refer to Web service log &A	Brute force password attack
Dialog logon	Critical	BUE	WS: Delayed logon successful (type &B, WP &C). Refer to Web service log &A	Brute force password attack
Dialog logon	Critical	BUI	SPNego replay attack detected (UPN=&A)	Denial of service or other repetitive command attack
Dialog logon	Critical	CU4	OAuth 2.0: Logged-on client user &A not same as parameter client ID &B	Hacker changed the logging
Dialog logon	Critical	CU6	OAuth 2.0: Client ID &A in SAML assertion not same as client ID &B in request	Hacker changed the logging
Dialog logon	Critical	DU0	Invalid SAP GUI data	External attack masquarading as SAP GUI

Audit class	Event class	Message ID	System log message text (before setting variables)	Cyber risk
Dialog logon	Severe	AU1	Logon successful (type=&A, method=&C)	Brute force password attack
Dialog logon	Severe	AUO	Logon failed (reason = &B, type = &A)	Brute force password attack
Dialog logon	Severe	CU2	OAuth 2.0: Invalid access token received (reason=&A)	Brute force password attack
Dialog logon	Severe	CU3	OAuth 2.0: Insufficient OAuth 2.0 scope for requested resource (user=&A)	Brute force password attack
Dialog logon	Severe	CU5	OAuth 2.0: Client &A requested invalid access grant type &B	Brute force password attack
Dialog logon	Severe	CU7	OAuth 2.0: Scope &B not permitted for client &C, user &D (cause=&A)	Brute force password attack
Dialog logon	Severe	CUA	Rejected Assertion	Password attack or code injection
Dialog logon	Severe	CUB	&A: &B	Password attack or code injection
Dialog logon	Severe	CUC	&A	Password attack or code injection
Dialog logon	Severe	CUD	Name ID of a subject	Password attack or code injection
Dialog logon	Severe	CUE	Attribute	Password attack or code injection
Dialog logon	Severe	CUF	Authentication Assertion	Hacker got into the system and was trying to break into other things
Dialog logon	Severe	CUG	Signed LogoutRequest rejected	Hacker got into the system as one id and tried logging out as another

Audit class	Event class	Message ID	System log message text (before setting variables)	Cyber risk
Dialog logon	Severe	CUH	Unsigned LogoutRequest rejected	Hacker accessed system as one ID and tried logging out as another
Dialog logon	Non-critical	AUC	User Logoff	Low risk
Dialog logon	Non-critical	BUK	&A assertion used	Low risk
Dialog logon	Non-critical	BUL	&A: &B	Low risk
Dialog logon	Non-critical	BUM	Name ID of a subject	Low risk
Dialog logon	Non-critical	BUN	Attribute	Low risk
Dialog logon	Non-critical	BUO	Authentication assertion	Low risk
Dialog logon	Non-critical	BUP	&A	Low risk
Dialog logon	Non-critical	BUQ	Signed LogoutRequest accepted	Low risk
Dialog logon	Non-critical	BUR	Unsigned LogoutRequest accepted	Low risk
Dialog logon	Non-critical	CU8	OAuth 2.0: Access token issued (client=&A, user=&B, grant type=&C)	Low risk
Dialog logon	Non-critical	CU9	OAuth 2.0: Valid access token received for user &A	Low risk
Other events	Critical	AUV	Digital signature error (reason = &A, ID = &B)	Password attack or code injection
Other events	Critical	BU0	RAL configuration access: Action: &A, type: &B, name &C	Hacker changing configuration

Audit class	Event class	Message ID	System log message text (before setting variables)	Cyber risk
Other events	Critical	BU1	Password check failed for user &B in client &A	Password attack or code injection
Other events	Critical	BU3	Security check changed in export: Old value &A, new value &B	Hacker changing configuration
Other events	Critical	BU8	Virus Scan Interface: Virus "&C" found by profile &A (step &B)	Virus
Other events	Critical	BUG	HTTP Security Session Management was deactivated for client &A	Hacker changing configuration
Other events	Critical	BUS	&A: Request without sufficient security characteristic of address &B	Hacker changing configuration
Other events	Critical	BUU	Certificate check for subject "&A" with profile &B failed (status &C)	Hacker changing configuration
Other events	Critical	BUY	Field contents changed: &5&9&9&9&9&9	Hacker changing configuration
Other events	Critical	BUZ	> in program &A, line &B, event &C	Hacker changing configuration
Other events	Critical	CU0	RAL Log Access: Action: &A	Code change/ injection
Other events	Critical	CUK	C debugging activated	Code change/ injection
Other events	Critical	CUL	Field content changed: &A	Code change/ injection
Other events	Critical	CUM	Jump to ABAP Debugger: &A	Code change/ injection
Other events	Critical	CUN	A manually caught process was stopped from within the Debugger (&A)	Code change/ injection

Audit class	Event class	Message ID	System log message text (before setting variables)	Cyber risk
Other events	Critical	CUO	Explicit database commit or rollback from debugger &A	Code change/ injection
Other events	Critical	CUP	Non-exclusive de-bugging session started	Code change/ injection
Other events	Critical	DUN	Active whitelist &A changed (&B)	Hacker changed the system whitelist logging
Other events	Critical	DUQ	Active scenario &A for switchable au-thorization checks changed – &B	Hacker changed the logging
Other events	Severe	AUY	Download &A Bytes to File &C	Code change/ injection
Other events	Severe	AUZ	Digital Signature (Rea-son = &A, ID = &B)	Code change/ injection
Other events	Severe	BU5	ICF recorder entry executed for user &A (activity &B)	Code change/ injection
Other events	Severe	BU6	ICF recorder entry executed by user &A (&B, &C) (activity &D)	Code change/ injection
Other events	Severe	BU7	Administration setting was changed for ICF Recorder (Activity: &A)	Hacker changing configuration
Other events	Severe	BU9	Virus Scan Interface: Error "&C" occurred in profile &A (step &B)	Hacker changing configuration
Other events	Severe	BUA	WS: Signature check error (reason &B, WP &C). Refer to Web service log &A	Code change/ injection
Other events	Severe	BUB	WS: Signature insufficient (WP &C). Refer to Web service log &A	Code change/ injection

Audit class	Event class	Message ID	System log message text (before setting variables)	Cyber risk
Other events	Severe	BUC	WS: Time stamp is invalid. Refer to Web service log &A	Code change/ injection
Other events	Severe	BUH	HTTP Security Session of user &A (client &B) was hard exited	Code change/ injection
Other events	Severe	BUJ	Non-encrypted &A communication (&B)	Code change/ injection
Other events	Severe	BUT	CRL download failed with error code &A	Code change/ injection
Other events	Severe	CU1	CU Test Message	Code change/ injection
Other events	Severe	CUQ	Logical file name &A not configured. Physical file name &B not checked.	Code change/ injection
Other events	Severe	CUR	Physical file name &B does not fulfill requirements from logical file name &A	Code change/ injection
Other events	Severe	CUS	Logical file name &B is not a valid alias for logical file name &A	Code change/ injection
Other events	Severe	CUT	Validation for logical file name &A is not active	Code change/ injection
Other events	Severe	DUA	EHS-SADM: Service &A created on host &B	Hacker changing configuration
Other events	Severe	DUB	EHS-SADM: Service &A started on host &B	Hacker changing configuration
Other events	Severe	DUC	EHS-SADM: Service &A ended on host &B	Hacker changing configuration
Other events	Severe	DUD	EHS-SADM: Service &A deleted on host &B	Hacker changing configuration

Audit class	Event class	Message ID	System log message text (before setting variables)	Cyber risk
Other events	Severe	DUM	Check for &A in whitelist &B failed	Hacker changing configuration
Other events	Severe	FU2	Parsing of an XML data stream canceled for security reasons (reason = &A)	Code change/ injection
Other events	Non-critical	AU0	Audit – Test. Text: &A	Low risk
Other events	Non-critical	BU4	Dynamic ABAP code: Event &A, event type &B, check total &C	Low risk
Other events	Non-critical	BUF	HTTP Security Session Management was activated for client &A.	Low risk
Other events	Non-critical	CUU	Payload of PI/WS message &A was read | &B	Low risk
Other events	Non-critical	CUX	Payload of post-processing request &A read	Low risk
Other events	Non-critical	CUY	> &A	Low risk
Other events	Non-critical	DUE	EHS-SADM: Configuration of service &A changed on host &B	Low risk
Other events	Non-critical	DUF	EHS-SADM: File &A transferred from host &B	Low risk
Other events	Non-critical	DUG	EHS-SADM: File &A transferred to host &B	Low risk
Other events	Non-critical	DUL	Check for &A in whitelist &B was successful	Low risk
Other events	Non-critical	DUO	Authorization check for object &A in scenario &B successful	Low risk

Audit class	Event class	Message ID	System log message text (before setting variables)	Cyber risk
Other events	Non-critical	DUP	Authorization check for object &A in scenario &B failed	Low risk
Other events	Non-critical	DUU	Authorization check for user &C on object &A in scenario &B successful	Low risk
Other events	Non-critical	DUV	Authorization check for user &C on object &A in scenario &B failed	Low risk
Other events	Non-critical	DUX	TEMP: Customer-specific event DUX &A &B &C &D	Low risk
Other events	Non-critical	DUY	TEMP: Customer-specific event DUY &A &B &C &D	Low risk
Other events	Non-critical	DUZ	TEMP: Customer-specific event DUZ &A &B &C &D	Low risk
Report start	Severe	AUX	Start of report &A Failed (reason = &B)	Low risk
Report start	Non-critical	AUW	Report &A started	Low risk
RFC Function Call	Critical	AUL	Failed RFC Call &C (Function Group = &A)	Code change/ injection
RFC Function Call	Critical	CUW	Failed Web service call (service = &A, operation = &B, reason = &C)	Code change/ injection
RFC Function Call	Critical	CUZ	Generic table access by RFC to &A with activity &B	Code change/ injection
RFC Function Call	Critical	DU3	Server &A is not contained in the whitelist	Hacker changing configuration

Audit class	Event class	Message ID	System log message text (before setting variables)	Cyber risk
RFC Function Call	Critical	DU4	Connection to server &A failed	Hacker changing configuration
RFC Function Call	Critical	DU5	There is no logical file name for path &A	Hacker changing configuration
RFC Function Call	Critical	DU7	Validation for &A failed	Hacker changing configuration
RFC Function Call	Critical	DUJ	RFC callback rejected (destination &A, called &B, callback &C)	Code change/ injection
RFC Function Call	Critical	DUK	RFC callback in simulation mode (destination &A, called &B, callback &C)	Code change/ injection
RFC Function Call	Critical	DUT	Critical JSON RPC call of function module &A (S_RFC * authorization)	Code change/ injection
RFC Function Call	Severe	DU1	FTP server whitelist is empty	Hacker changing configuration
RFC Function Call	Severe	DU2	FTP server whitelist is non-secure due to use of placeholders	Hacker changing configuration
RFC Function Call	Non-critical	AUK	Successful RFC call &C (Function Group = &A)	
RFC Function Call	Non-critical	CUV	Successful WS Call (service = &A, operation &B)	
RFC Function Call	Non-critical	DU6	Validation for &A successful	
RFC Function Call	Non-critical	DU8	FTP connection request for server &A successful	

Audit class	Event class	Message ID	System log message text (before setting variables)	Cyber risk
RFC Function Call	Non-critical	DUI	RFC callback executed (destination &A, called &B, callback &C)	
RFC Function Call	Non-critical	DUR	JSON RPC call of function module &A succeeded	
RFC Function Call	Non-critical	DUS	JSON RPC call of function module &A failed	
RFC Function Call	Non-critical	FU1	RFC function &B with dynamic destination &C was called in program &A	
RFC/CPIC Logon	Critical	AU6	RFC/CPIC logon failed, reason=&B, type=&A, method=&C	
RFC/CPIC Logon	Non-critical	AU5	RFC/CPIC logon successful (type=&A, method=&C)	
System	Critical	AUE	Audit Configuration Changed	Hacker changing configuration
System	Critical	AUF	Audit: Slot &A: Class &B, Severity &C, User &D, Client &E, &F	Hacker changing configuration
System	Critical	AUG	Application Server Started	Code change/ injection
System	Critical	AUH	Application Server Stopped	Code change/ injection
System	Critical	AUI	Audit: Slot &A Inactive	Hacker changing configuration
System	Critical	AUJ	Audit: Active Status Set to &1	Hacker changing configuration
System	Critical	EU1	System changeability changed (&A to &B)	Hacker changing configuration

Audit class	Event class	Message ID	System log message text (before setting variables)	Cyber risk
System	Critical	EU2	Client setting for &A changed (&B)	Hacker changing configuration
Transaction Start	Critical	AU4	Start of transaction &A failed (Reason=&B)	Code change/ injection
Transaction Start	Critical	CUJ	Failed to start application &A (reason =&B)	Code change/ injection
Transaction Start	Severe	AUP	Transaction &A locked	Code change/ injection
Transaction Start	Severe	AUQ	Transaction &A Unlocked	Code change/ injection
Transaction Start	Severe	BUX	Test message	Code change/ injection
Transaction Start	Non-critical	AU3	Transaction &A Started	
Transaction Start	Non-critical	CUI	Application &A started	
Transaction Start	Non-critical	DU9	Generic table access call to &A with activity &B (auth. check: &C)	
User Master Record Change	Critical	AU7	User &A Created	Hacker changing configuration, creating / changing users for access
User Master Record Change	Critical	AUU	&A &B activated	Hacker changing configuration, creating / changing users for access
User Master Record Change	Critical	BUV	Invalid hash value &A. The context contains &B	Hacker changing configuration, creating / changing users for access

Audit class	Event class	Message ID	System log message text (before setting variables)	Cyber risk
User Master Record Change	Critical	BUW	A refresh token issued to client &A was used by client &B	Hacker changing configuration, creating / changing users for access
User Master Record Change	Severe	AU8	User &A Deleted	Hacker changing configuration, creating / changing users to hide trail
User Master Record Change	Severe	AU9	User &A Locked	Hacker changing configuration, creating / changing users for access
User Master Record Change	Severe	AUA	User &A Unlocked	Hacker changing configuration, creating / changing users for access
User Master Record Change	Severe	AUB	Authorizations for User &A Changed	Hacker changing configuration, creating / changing users for access
User Master Record Change	Severe	AUD	User Master Record &A Changed	Hacker changing configuration, creating / changing users for access
User Master Record Change	Severe	AUR	A& &B created	Hacker changing configuration, creating / changing users for access
User Master Record Change	Severe	AUS	A& &B deleted	Hacker changing configuration, creating / changing users for access

Audit class	Event class	Message ID	System log message text (before setting variables)	Cyber risk
User Master Record Change	Severe	AUT	A& &B changed	Hacker changing configuration, creating / changing users for access
User Master Record Change	Severe	DUH	OAuth 2.0: Token declared invalid (OAuth client=&A, user=&B, token type=&C)	Hacker changing configuration, creating / changing users for access
User Master Record Change	Non-critical	BU2	Password changed for user &B in client &A	

You have finished the book.

Sign up for our newsletter!

Stay up to date!

Sign up for our newsletter for updates on new SAP book releases and exclusive discounts.

http://newsletter.espresso-tutorials.com.

A The Author

Julie Hallett has a Masters Degree in Cybersecurity Policy, is a Certified Information Systems Security Professional (CISSP) and is Certified in Risk and Information Systems (CRISC) Controls. She has over 20 years' experience in Information Technology, Enterprise Systems Architecture, SAP Security Architecture, Cybersecurity, Governance, Risk, and Compliance, and Information Assurance in complex landscapes with numerous integration issues.

Julie is an expert in security frameworks and was one of the first SAP customer researchers and speakers in the application of cybersecurity programs and frameworks for SAP Enterprise Architecture. She has been an SAP TechEd and dCode, SAP GRC and SAP Cyber Conference speaker for over 10 years and is a subject matter expert in the area of cybersecurity. Julie can be contacted at julshallett@gmail.com.

B Index

C Disclaimer

This publication contains references to the products of SAP SE.

SAP, R/3, SAP NetWeaver, Duet, PartnerEdge, ByDesign, SAP Business-Objects Explorer, StreamWork, and other SAP products and services mentioned herein as well as their respective logos are trademarks or registered trademarks of SAP SE in Germany and other countries.

Business Objects and the Business Objects logo, BusinessObjects, Crystal Reports, Crystal Decisions, Web Intelligence, Xcelsius, and other Business Objects products and services mentioned herein as well as their respective logos are trademarks or registered trademarks of Business Objects Software Ltd. Business Objects is an SAP company.

Sybase and Adaptive Server, iAnywhere, Sybase 365, SQL Anywhere, and other Sybase products and services mentioned herein as well as their respective logos are trademarks or registered trademarks of Sybase, Inc. Sybase is an SAP company.

SAP SE is neither the author nor the publisher of this publication and is not responsible for its content. SAP Group shall not be liable for errors or omissions with respect to the materials. The only warranties for SAP Group products and services are those that are set forth in the express warranty statements accompanying such products and services, if any. Nothing herein should be construed as constituting an additional warranty.

More Espresso Tutorials Books

Maxim Chuprunov:

Leveraging SAP® GRC in the Fight Against Corruption and Fraud

- ▶ Overview of classic SAP ABAP interface techniques
- ▶ Design and implement an anti-corruption initiative
- ▶ Automated drivers and added value GRC
- ▶ Detection scenarios using SAP Fraud Management and SAP HANA

http://5216.espresso-tutorials.com/

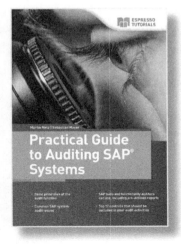

Martin Metz, Sebastian Mayer:

Practical Guide to Auditing SAP® Systems

- ▶ Basic principles of the audit function
- ▶ Common SAP system audit issues
- ▶ SAP tools and functionality auditors can use, including pre-defined reports
- ▶ Top 12 controls that should be included in your audit activities

http://5248.espresso-tutorials.com

Bert Vanstechelman, Chris Walravens, Christophe Decamps:

Securing SAP® S/4HANA

- ▶ Effectively secure SAP S/4HANA, Fiori, and Gateway
- ▶ Privileges and roles, authentication, encryption, and monitoring
- ▶ Mobile access and SSO considerations
- ▶ Cross-system authorization concepts and implementation

http://5258.espresso-tutorials.com

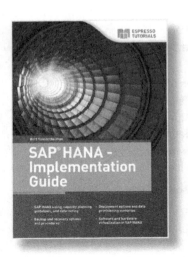

Bert Vanstechelman:

The SAP® HANA Implementation Guide

- ▶ SAP HANA sizing, capacity planning guidelines, and data tiering
- ▶ Deployment options and data provisioning scenarios
- ▶ Backup and recovery options and procedures
- ▶ Software and hardware virtualization in SAP HANA

http://5289.espresso-tutorials.com

Tracy Juran:

Beginner's Guide to SAP® Security and Authorizations

- ▶ Basic architecture of SAP Security and Authorizations
- ▶ GRC Access Control introduction
- ▶ User profile creation and role assignments
- ▶ Common security and authorization pain point troubleshooting

http://5013.espresso-tutorials.com

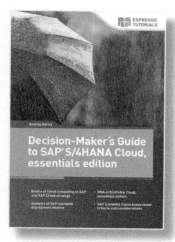

Anurag Barua:

Decision-Maker's Guide to SAP® S/4HANA Cloud, essentials edition

- ▶ Basics of cloud computing in SAP and SAP Cloud strategy
- ▶ Analysis of SAP S/4HANA deployment models
- ▶ DNA of S/4HANA Cloud, essentials edition
- ▶ SAP S/4HANA Cloud assessment criteria and considerations

http://5424.espresso-tutorials.com

Made in the USA
Las Vegas, NV
03 May 2024

89502305R00085